SUCCESSFUL WRITING

EDUCATION AND HUMAN COMMUNICATION SERIES

PUBLISH OR PERISH: A guide
for academic authors
Edited by P.J.Hills

SUCCESSFUL WRITING
Nancy Harrison

UCCESSFUL

WRITING

Nancy Harrison

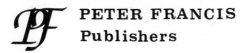 PETER FRANCIS
Publishers

© 1987 Nancy Harrison

Peter Francis Publishers, Orchard House,
Berrycroft, Soham Ely. Cambs.. CB7 5BL

British Library Cataloguing in Publication Data

Harrison, Nancy
  Successful writing. - (Education and
  human communication).
  1. Authorship
  I. Title   II. Series
  808'.02   PN146

  ISBN 1-870167-00-7

Printed and bound in Great Britain by
Biddles Ltd, Guildford and Kings Lynn

CONTENTS

Contents

Contents

INTRODUCTION

The Purpose of this Book

The subject of this book is written English. As the word **writing** seems to imply, to some faint-hearts, an action beyond their capabilities, it will be defined by me as marks made on paper or other markable material (including fences, walls and motorway bridges) by pens, typewriters, word-processors and aerosol sprays to convey information. The writing to be dealt with is **prose.** Do not, at this point, shut the book. Prose comprises all written work other than poetry, and it stretches all the way from "Kilroy was Here" to Gibbon's "Decline and Fall of the Roman Empire".

The word **writer** will be used. This term is often confused with **author.** For my purpose the writer is any person who puts words down on paper, whether the words merely ask a neighbour to turn his radio down or communicate to a startled world a re-markable new theory about fleas. Writers may become authors but it is not compulsory and few do so. Certainly, they cannot do so unless they have learnt to control the medium of expression, writing.

The written language is based on the same elements as speech. In theory, it should be acquired just as naturally. But certain factors militate against

Introduction

this ease of mastery. Spoken English varies from place to place, area to area and country to country. Dialects and regional variations contain idiomatic expressions and usages. One person's colloquial speech is often unintelligible to another; colloquial speech fails to provide a universal means of communication.

Written language, on the other hand, has rules and guidelines which, despite minor variations in the major English-using countries, enable meaning to be conveyed from user to user without hindrance. Broad syntactical principles extend the comprehension of English across frontiers. The Yorkshire businessman can write to clients in the Isle of Wight and in Singapore with equal certainty of understanding, and the novel written by an author in Kansas City may be enjoyed by a Hebridean crofter.

A Word in your Eye

Written communication is different from spoken communication; you can't hear it. A great many people believe that they have only to put words on paper just as they would say them and their ideas will be instantly understood by any reader. The Creative English classes at school may well have encouraged this belief, the more so if they have never encountered any other teaching on written language. It must be discouraging to have been told at the age of twelve that one's outpourings are "very good, Fred", only to find at the advanced age of nineteen that one's university tutor thinks they are garbled garbage.

Any book on the subject of written English tends to be regarded as a means of learning how to write a novel, preferably one of 300,000 words with a strong story-formula that will guarantee its

Introduction

appearance on every airport bookstall. It might also teach one to write poetry or short stories for women's magazines. But it is a false concept because it divides written work into two classes. The first, "creative" writing, is theoretically work of imagination: writing stories or poetry. In practice the classroom activity consists of recording activities or thoughts just as they come into the writer's head, to be accepted without criticism or guidance in case the "creative flow" is discouraged. The second class of writing, it is assumed, is the everyday stuff of notes, memoranda, research papers, reports, letters, essays and anything that is written in connection with one's studies or work.

This is really idealistic nonsense. There is as much creativity in writing to one's bank manager or composing a letter about faulty goods as in any classroom set piece. Anyone whose creative flow was ruined forever because someone said that their work would be improved by better punctuation had little creative flow to start with. If Johnson and Milton, Jane Austen and Dickens, Georgette Heyer and William Golding survived severer criticism than any found in the classroom of today with creative flow intact, then learning the use of good written English cannot harm anyone.

To write as the fancy takes one, but without an adequate vocabulary or a competence in language structure, is pointless. There must be an understanding of the generally-accepted rules of language if anyone other than the writer and an indulgent teacher is to make sense of what is written. In a cloud-cuckoo world we could dispense with form and regulation in writing. We could also have the milk without the bottle, chocolate without the wrapper and spaghetti sauce without the tin. There would be a mess, but one shared by all the world.

Introduction

However, in the real world, what is written needs to be comprehensible by any reader. That reader, moreover, may be someone unknown who will judge the writer by what is written. Abandoning clarity might have a decisive effect on the writer's future. For some reason the teaching profession seem to overlook the fact that a young engineer who cannot understand the structure of language when he needs to produce written work may have been disadvantaged by the school curriculum. Everybody needs to be able to write simply and coherently at the same time. A young person leaving school without any knowledge of grammar and syntax has been robbed of a vital part of his or her heritage.

Fortunately for us all, language is really quite easy. If we can learn to comprehend speech, so we can learn to write. A simple mastery over the mechanics of writing should be the goal. To achieve this, there is no need to enter the typographical complexities of linguistics. A disciplined approach to the subject and an understanding of the way in which words are put together to convey meaning are all that is required.

1 WORDS ACROSS SPACE AND TIME

An Unsecret Code

It is obvious that when messages cannot be spoken,
or even shouted, because the message-receiver is
not in the same place at the same time as the
message-sender, there must be a visible or
tangible way of presenting them. Written language
is merely a code-system, capable of variation in
order to convey messages of differing complexity.
The code system involves vocabulary, grammar and
syntax, terms which sound difficult. Technical
terms will not, however, bite you and can be
understood quite easily if we think of them as
friendly. We have no trouble in realising that
"increment", a mathematical term, means more money
in the wage-packet or better-looking figures on
the salary-cheque.

Vocabulary is the collective term for the words we
use to describe things, states and actions.
Grammar is the science, or study, of language,
dealing with all languages, the words in them and
the interactions of those words. **Syntax** deals with
the way in which words are put together to express
thoughts and ideas sensibly. The most important
parts of the code for the simple business of
writing good English are vocabulary and syntax.
You need to know, or to be able to find, the right
words to describe what is in your mind. Further,

Words across Space and Time

since words by themselves are only descriptive of individual things, states or actions, you must learn to put them together to make sense of the message you seek to convey.

A Sense of Purpose

One of the most unhelpful pieces of information one can come across is the notice on a shop door which reads "BACK IN TEN MINUTES". It could have been put there one minute ago or nine minutes ago; it might have been put there an hour ago, even yesterday, and forgotten; perhaps it is not meant for a customer, but rather for the owner's wife, the bailiffs or the cat. Because it is so vague - after all, it does not even tell you who expects to be back in ten minutes - the luckless customer must weigh up the advantages of standing around for ten minutes or going elsewhere. As a communication it is as useful as a broken rubber band.

Any written communication has an underlying purpose. If there is no reason to write, just putting marks on paper is a waste of time. The purpose of everyday communication is to inform someone of something. Information is knowledge passed from one person to another. Even the act of informing yourself about a subject consists of consulting another person or reading something written by another person. The amount of in- formation passed may be great or small and it may also include two elements: information about the subject and information about yourself.

Whatever the nature of information passed, it always comprises facts, thoughts or ideas. A lie is a fact and therefore as much a part of information as the truth; if someone has been misinformed they may have been given bad

Words across Space and Time

information but it is information nevertheless.
How reliable the information is may be a matter
for conjecture, but it is still something passed
from one person to another.

At a fundamental level, what needs to be said can
often be stated very simply: FLOOD and TRY YOUR
BRAKES, CLOSED ALL DAY WEDNESDAY and NO SPITTING.
Basic information in simple statements can be
aimed at a general audience or readership: FALLING
ROCKS; or specific groups: NO DOGS; or individuals: YOUR SUPPER IS IN THE OVEN. They are
usually practical in intention, if not always so
in wording. NO EXIT on the street side of a door
makes one wonder what one should do on emerging
from the door. Should one go back in and find
another door through which to leave? Or should one
just sneak off down the street hoping that no one
has seen one coming out?

All Will Be Explained

Practical information often needs to be expanded.
Reasons and details are given to clarify and
explain the basic information. Explanation ensures
that there is no gap in understanding between what
is written and what is read. The handbook that
arrives with an elaborate piece of domestic
equipment ought to explain exactly how the machine
works. Examination questions often require the
student to explain the answer or give details to
support the worth of what is said.

Esays and, at a higher academic level, papers for
conferences and articles for journals are examples
of exposition. They not only describe and explain
but also interpret. What is put down must be
pertinent to the subject and expand the reader's
knowledge or understanding of a subject within his
or her discipline or occupation; in the case of

the tutor, who knows more than you do, it must demonstrate your grasp of the subject. The presentation of a paper can be very difficult for someone whose technical or scientific training has not included education in the use of written English. Too often the desperate presenter plumps out generalized statements wih a huff and puff of irrelevant jargon in order to meet a desired length, relying on questions from the audience to winkle out the information he undoubtedly has. Unfortunately, papers of this sort are meant to be suitable for publication and badly-written ones are a waste of paper. An inability to put things in writing is a form of illiteracy, however highly trained one may be in other ways.

It follows from this that you must have clearly in mind the reasons for writing, knowing **why** you are writing something. That reason involves two other factors: for whom something is written and what you need to say.

It Takes Two to Communicate

Writing is essentially a dialogue. The act of writing something down shows that it is meant to be seen. This is true even of something as transient as a reminder to yourself to speak to the laundryman or as private as a diary. They are there to be consulted by one's later or older self. In written work you are always the principal speaker but you would not be speaking, or rather writing, were it not for the reader, the hearer of what you say. In other words, communication depends on a giver of information and someone to receive it. The person receiving is just as important in the art of writing as the person putting the words down on paper.

General information and simple statements of the

sort already quoted are usually aimed at people not known to the writer. For the purpose of this book, however, it must be assumed that if you do not know by name the person for whom you write, you are nonetheless aware of what is expected from you.

What you write tells the reader something about you. It is an expression of self. This is most apparent in the exposition of a subject, when the writer describes and interprets for an audience already familiar with at least some aspects of the subject. It is important for students to realise that essays display to tutors the degree of understanding they have reached. In the same way, a report written for an employer or the head of a department is not only a report on the subject but also a report on yourself.

This need to fit what you write to the requirements of your reader also applies to written reports. In any hierarchical est-ablishment, a large company or civil service department, senior members need information provided by people working in specialized sections. The clearer and more succinct the report, the more useful it will be and, consequently, the greater the respect for the writer.

But there are dangers. Whether you are writing for an employer, a tutor or an examiner, never be tempted to show off. They know more than you do, like good cooks who can recognize a gobbling turkey and have refuse bins full of bones to prove it.

Determining the identity of your partner in communication, the reader, is important. It should enable you to decide what information that reader needs to have.

Words Across Space and Time

Not too Much and Not too Little

As writing is really codified speech, it could be argued that what you would say to someone on a subject would be as comprehensible when set down on paper. If this were true, it would be equally valid to argue that bears should be employed as bee-keepers because they are good at honey-gathering in the wild. In codifying a message we should improve understanding. There is no way of including the soundless parts of spoken communication. Hesitations and digressions are lost; there are no hand-movements or shoulders shrugged; smiles, pursed lips and raised eyebrows cannot be coded. The written message stands on its words alone.

The content of the message, then, is what matters. Given the subject, you must determine what needs to be said about it. Only then do you decide what further information must be given to clarify or round out that information.

The form or nature of the communication dictates the way in which it is written. The form may be limiting. If you are asked to précis or summarize a longer statement or passage, you should be aware that this involves cutting out or removing all but the essential facts contained in the original work. When you see the words "briefly" or "in not more than --- words" you know that the length is preset. In some circumstances, however, you must be prepared to limit yourself.

When a note or memorandum is required, it must be short and to the point. If you are writing to the Inspector of Taxes there is no need to tell him about your grandmother's corns, unless the amount you have spent on her cornplasters is an allowable expense. Answering an examination question calls for the same sort of self-restraint. Remember that you will only get credit for the answer to the question - not for the answers to the questions you wish you had been asked.

The brief communications consists of the facts stripped of unnecessary trimmings. It is harder to write at length with as much cogency. Any subject is part of a much wider subject. The difficulty lies in deciding where to draw the limits of what can reasonably be included. If one solitary dinosaur were discovered to be living on the shores of a wild Finnish lake, it would be natural and sensible to refer to its long-dead relations to establish the importance of the discovery. A two-headed camel is remarkable only because most camels have but one head.

Whether the subject is a computer or a novelist, the context in which you choose to place it is relevant. To give the entire history of computation and its electronic advancement, or the world-wide development of prose fiction, every time that computers or novelists were written about would be superfluous and very boring. It is necessary to be selective.

Some of the additional material needed to illustrate your dissertation or argument will present itself. If you are examining the work of certain 19th century novelists, including Scott and Dickens, certain common factors exist: the reading habits of the Victorian public, the nature of the publishing industry at the time, the popularity of part-works and so on. The work can then be made more interesting by particularizing, giving details of the personal circumstances in which each novelist had to work and how this affected their output. On the other hand, if you are writing about just one novelist, Jane Austen, for example, you must choose whether you will look at her work in its historical context, whether you

will compare her work with that of another
novelist or whether you will examine the way in
which her environment and private life affected
her writing.

When you are writing a report or preparing a paper
for your department, your company or a conference,
you must be just as selective. Decisions must be
made about details that contribute or are unnecessary. The Board may be well aware of the
company structure and the reasons for pursuing a
particular marketing course. What they want to
know are the measures of progress and success.
They may not want to know about short-comings and
failure but your brief may require you to tell
them. The audience (and, by extension, the
readership) to whom your paper is addressed is
almost certainly familiar with the current state
of the profession, discipline or technology you
share. The need is to be informed of what is new,
and only those facts which bear on the innovation
or advance are relevant.

Getting to Work

It is not the function of this book to teach you
how to write. You alone know the sort of clothes
you feel comfortable in and the sort of food you
like to eat. Jam and oysters may not be everyone's
favourite combination but they may be yours.
Writing is an aspect of personality in just the
same way. The way in which you express yourself on
paper is as individual as your choice of clothes
or taste in food.

What can be acquired is a working method, one
which enables you to marshal your ideas in good
order. Because it must suit you, you will have to
discover it by trial and error. Having said that,
the preliminary work for anything other than a

Words Across Space and Time

bald instruction must be simple and to the point.

Parts, Tools and Equipment

A vast array of words at your beck and call is less important than a knowledge of the meaning and worth of the words you already know. That does not mean that you need not increase your vocabulary. On the contrary, being able to choose from a number of words the right one for your purpose is a necessary requirement for clear communication. You should, by reading and using dictionaries, enlarge your store of words as often as you can.

The use to which words are put and the way in which they are joined together are of paramount importance in writing well.

> ... I came to the conclusion that
> they must all be näive of his
> actions and are naive to CND.

This writer starts his dismal catalogue of errors by failing to understand the word "naive". The dictionary tells us that it means "artless, unaffected, amusingly simple", which seems pretty harmless. In the sentence quoted it is misused to mean "gullible; foolishly trusting", a not uncommon misuse. Not content with ignorant mis-usage, the writer then stuffs in two prepositions to which this unassuming adjective "naive" is not entitled. Even had he used the word "gullible", the prepositions "of" and "to" would still make nonsense of the sentence.

The order of words can be as important as the meaning and nature of the words themselves.

13

> Mr --- --- seems to suffer from more
> misconceptions than he claims others to
> have

With some effort, we can see what the writer
means. But he has strayed all over the place in
getting there. Perhaps his typewriter ran away
with him; certainly, he does not seem to have read
through his letter before sending it to the
newspapers. If the second half of the sentence
read "than he claims for others" it would be
improved.

Because syntax, the mechanics of sentence
construction, lies at the heart of good writing,
we must start there. The next two chapters will
look at words and how they are linked for the
purpose of communication.

2 THE RAW MATERIALS

Words and More Words

Words are the essence of communication. Even sign
language is based on descriptive terms for things
and actions. Yet words by themselves have meaning
but no sense. Take successive words from the
dictionary: abbot, abbreviate, ABC, abdicate, for
example. Although each one is given a definition,
they have no relationship to each other. To make
sense, or nonsense, of them they must be sparked
up with other words:

> The abbott, who abbreviated the
> ABC, recently abdicated.

Move further into the dictionary and find another
group of words: hippocras, Hippocratic oath,
Hippocrene, hippodrome, hippogryph and hippo-
potamus.

> Drunk on hippocras, he took the
> Hippocratic oath in a Hippocrene-
> induced daze before breaking his
> neck at the hippodrome while trying
> to race a hippogryph against a
> hippopotamus.

Both these sentences come under the heading of

The Raw Materials

Creative Writing and have no material value
whatever.

Obviously, there must be some distinction between
words used for different purposes. Some only
describe or designate. Others provide direction or
action for those that only describe, while yet
more qualify or join. All are important in themselves but are more important in their co-
operation. They have to work together to be
effective elements of communication.

It is worth examining the nature of the different
sorts of words. By doing so, the parts they play
in establishing the meaning of what is written
become clearer. The ways in which they must be
related lie in the functions they perform.

Names for Everything

A **noun** is defined as the name of a person or
thing. It is sometimes called a **substantive.** Both
the alternative name and the definition do less
than justice to nouns. They are the words for the
tangible and intangible, for what is seen and what
is unseen, for things of the spirit and of the
flesh, for popes, prelates, pirates and ordinary
people.

The naming function of nouns must cover every
object or concept, whether material or spiritual,
concrete or imaginary. Anything we can see, feel
or think about is named. The named thing need not
be real; concepts as disparate as locomotives and
dreams are nameable. The noun, in naming, does not
establish the reality or validity of things or
ideas - the name is just a label. An armadillo
remains an armadillo even if you mistakenly call
it a tulip or a pork pie.

The Raw Materials

For the sake of order, nouns are divided into four main groups

Common nouns describe objects in a general way as belonging to a group of objects:
     table, tree, tuba, turnip.

Abstract nouns name states, qualities and actions that are not visible or tangible:
     humour, temper, silence, misery.

Proper nouns label people, places or things in particular:
     Mabel, Madrid, the Maritime Museum.

Collective nouns, with **nouns of multitude,** describe collections or groups of things or people:
     pile, crowd, jury, herd.

Plurals and Awkward Irregularities

When there is more than one thing to be considered we use a plural noun. Most plurals are formed by adding 's' or 'es' to the end of the word. 'Boy' becomes 'boys', 'box' becomes 'boxes'. Some remember their ancient origins with a suffix: children, oxen, brethren. Other things change their form, or mutate: 'goose' to 'geese', 'mouse' to 'mice' and 'man' to 'men'. These are familiar words and few people make mistakes in using them.

More difficult are those words which have no singular form. Is half a 'pair of scissors' a 'scissor'? Can one say that one leg of a 'pair of pants' or 'trousers' is a 'pant' or 'trouser'? If there were any justice, one might think so, but it is an unfair world. 'Pants', 'trousers' and 'scissors' are forever plural and will take a plural verb, like 'entrails' and 'tweezers'.

The Raw Materials

Some words seem to be plural but are treated as singular: 'mumps', 'measles' and 'mathematics'.

    Mumps are painful

is wrong; so is

    A measle is itchy.

In a sentence such as

    Mumps and measles are both diseases
    of childhood

we have a sentence with two subjects so the verb is rightly plural; but in

    measles is a serious disease

we need a singular verb. It is right to say

    mathematics is my worst subject

or

    gymnastics is a popular sport.

But there is one sense in which both words are plural. When they are regarded as subjects of parts (mathematics comprises trigonometry, calculus and other subjects) a reference to some of the parts calls for a plural verb form. So we say

    the higher mathematics are
    important in technical education

or

    gymnastics are exercises to improve the body.

The Raw Materials

Check your usage when dealing with other words of this sort:

metaphysics, ethics, athletics

and so on. 'Politics', however, are always plural.

Some familiar nouns have the same form in both singular and plural:

sheep, deer, stone(weight), dozen, etc.

Others can trip one up because they sound singular but are, in fact, plural:

swine, cattle, vermin, etc.

Differentiate between the herd of snuffling pink pigs and the swine who takes your parking place; the pejorative term is singular.

There are also nouns which are unfailingly singular and have no plural form. Do not be tempted to give them one.

furniture	gout
scenery	laziness
courage	conduct
demeanour	sloth (deadly sin)
poetry	behaviour*

(*'behaviours' is sometimes used by psychologists as a pseudo-technical term, but it has no place in the general vocabulary)

19

The Raw Materials

The **Collective Nouns**, even though they represent a number of things or people, are treated as singular when the collection is considered as a whole.

A **skein** of geese was seen overhead.

The **jury** is still sitting.

The **crowd** was angry.

The **herd** stands in one corner of the field.

When, on the other hand, the individuals making up the group are considered, the word becomes plural.

The **jury** are restless.

The **crowd** were shouting and throwing stones.

The **herd** are scattering.

Be quite sure of the sense you intend. The nouns in the second list of examples are **nouns of multitude**, a term which distinguishes their plural form. Although most of these words can be used as either collective nouns or nouns of multitude, you must never mix the usage. Be consistent. **Parliament** cannot be referred to as singular in one sentence and transferred into a plural in the next.

Plural Puzzles - the Anomalous Nouns

Anomalous, in the sense in which these nouns are described, means abnormal. They look like one kind of noun but behave, deceptively, like another.

'Riches', 'eaves' and 'alms', for instance, are really singular nouns. The 's' is part of the word; 'riches' comes from 'richesse', 'alms' is derived from 'almysse' and 'eaves' began as 'efes'.
All three are nevertheless treated as plurals.

'Tones', 'trappings' and 'thanks' are genuinely plural, lacking singular forms. Imagine yourself giving one thank.

But 'news', 'means' and 'innings' are plurals treated as if they were singular.

'Summons' is singular; the correct plural 'summones'.

'Gallows' has no such refinement. It is singular but two or more gallows are plural without change of spelling.

Number

It is necessary to consider whether nouns are singular or plural because of their relationship with other words in a sentence. A singular noun takes a singular verb; plural nouns take plural verbs. This matching of noun and verb is **agreement.** The verb agrees with the **number** of the noun.

Gender

Inanimate things, in English, are regarded as sexless. They are of the **neuter gender.** Don't be misled by the fanciful concept of ships and countries as masculine or feminine. Grammatically, only if a word specifically indicates that some-

The Raw Materials

The distinction only scrapes an existence in English. The somewhat rare differences in words that apply to human beings indicate some special advantage or quality. The difference between an **actor** and an **actress** is that he is cast in the role of Li'l Abner while she plays the part of Daisy Mae. It is also useful to distinguish between 'aunts' and 'uncles', 'husbands' and 'wives', 'brothers' and 'sisters'. Feminizing words by adding '-ess' is totally unnecessary. If work is done, it matters little whether it was well or ill done by a woman or a man. The practice, still sometimes seen, of adding a feminine prefix to a word, as in 'lady-taxidriver' or 'lady-superintendant', is an outmoded genteelism, better forgotten.

In the zoological and agricultural world, there are a number of instances of quite different words to differentiate between males and females of a species:

> 'gander' and 'goose',
> 'pen' and 'cob' (swans)   and
> 'bull' and 'cow'.

Apart from the practicality of such distinctions, their significance to the writer lies in the choice of **pronoun.** As we shall see later, gender is a more serious consideration when pronouns are used.

Case

Before we tackle the subject of pronouns, there is the matter of case. The subject of a sentence is always in the **subjective case**; it is the person or thing to which the verb is primarily related. The subject is what the sentence is· about. It is the

The Raw Materials

word that commands the sentence. Mr Circumspex, in

        Mr Circumspex hailed a taxi

is the subject, but what of the taxi? In all but
the simplest statements, the subject is related,
through the verb, to an object, in this case the
taxi. The person or thing that is on the receiving
end of the sentence is in the **objective case.**

In English, nouns have lost that convenient
capacity to change shape or spelling to show
whether they are the subject or the object. The
position of the word in the sentence usually
indicates its case. But the fact that there is no
obvious change in a word does not mean that we can
dismiss its case as irrelevant. The more words
there are in a sentence, the more important it
becomes to be able to identify the object.

Although nouns have no visible objective case, the
next group of words to be considered, the
pronouns, do change to show case. As pronouns
require a **noun antecedent,** the part that a noun
plays in the sentence must be known.

However, before tackling pronouns, there is one
case that affects nouns which can be seen: the
possessive. This, the case of ownership, is based
on convenience. It is cumbersome to say or write

        the umbrella of Mr Circumspex.

Instead we use an **apostrophe** and 's' to give Mr
Circumspex his pronoun:

        Mr. Circumspex's umbrella.

Convenient this system may be, but it poses some
awkward questions:

The Raw Materials

What do we do with plural possessives?
What happens if the word already ends in 's'?

If the plural noun does not end in 's', the form
is the same as for the singular:

>   sheep's eyes,
>   children's books.

If the plural ends in 's', which is far commoner,
we only add an apostrophe after the 's':

>   bridegrooms' buttonholes,
>   foxes' earths.

But if the singular noun ends in 's', it is given
the full treatment, an apostrophe and an 's':

>   the census's figures,
>   the pass's difficulties.

This applies particularly to proper nouns, both
well-known and obscure:

>   Dickens's novels;
>   Mr. Circumspex has his umbrella, but
>   where are Charles's and Silenus's?

Personal and Impersonal Pointers - Pronouns

The pronouns that first catch our attention are,
naturally, those that concern us personally and
concern any others fortunate enough to be included
with us: I, me, we, us. These are followed by the
pronouns that refer to other people, things or
animals: he, him, she, her, they, them. Lastly,
there is the neuter pronoun: it, and its plural:
them.

To save tedious repetitions of the same words and

The Raw Materials

make statements shorter, we often substitute an appropriate pronoun for a noun after its first appearance.

> Mr Circumspex worked because **he** liked making money.

They are convenient but they have one absolute requirement. Every pronoun must refer to something else that has either already appeared in the statement or is implicitly identified. 'I', 'you' and 'we' speak for themselves; they represent the person or persons addressing some other person or persons, and the person or persons addressed. That to which reference is made is the **antecedent** of the pronoun. Because pronouns are among the most muddled and misused words, the need for an antecedent should be in every pronoun-user's mind.

Different types of pronouns perform different functions.

> **Personal pronouns** represent the identity of a person or thing;

> **Possessive pronouns** express ownership or command of something;

> **Relative pronouns** join statements and identify the subjects and objects of clauses;

> **Demonstrative pronouns** point things out;

> **Interrogative pronouns** question identity;

> **Indefinite and negative pronouns** express doubt and negation;

> **Reflexive pronouns** emphasize identity.

The Raw Materials

Before examining the way in which pronouns differ
in their actions, we must see the way in which
they reflect the nouns for which they are
substitutes.

Pronouns, Case and Number

Nouns may not change to display their subjective
or objective nature. Pronouns do. Personal
pronouns, for instance, change dramatically.

Singular

	1st person	2nd person	3rd person
Subjective	I	you	he, she, it
Objective	me	you	him, her, it

Plural

Subjective	we	you	they
Objective	us	you	them

Possessive pronouns always display their possessive nature; the form of the word shows ownership:
the possessive case.

Singular

1st person	2nd person	3rd person
my	your	his, her, its

Plural

our	your	their

All the pronouns in that list are adjectival and
are always followed by a noun.

> In the rain, Mr Circumspex opens
> his umbrella.

The Raw Materials

The word 'his' is effectively an adjective describing the umbrella. The pronoun that acts as a pronoun should do, taking the place of a noun, is the 'double possessive'.

Singular

1st person	2nd person	3rd person
mine	yours	his,hers,its

Plural

ours	yours	theirs

Like other pronouns, the double possessive needs an antecedent because it refers to a noun:

> Mrs Circumspex picked up his
> umbrella but left hers behind.

The object belonging to this woman, who is either careless or self-sacrificing, is, and must be from the sense, an umbrella.

Muddied Waters

It may seem foolish to list words that are so much a part of everyday usage. Unfortunately, there are many people who find it difficult to distinguish between the subjective and objective forms. There is a vague feeling that the accusative form is somehow ungenteel or derogatory and, as the position of the pronoun does not always indicate its relationship to the subject, it is better to play safe and use the subjective:

> After an argument, the doorman allowed
> Mr Circumspex and I to leave.

The Raw Materials

This is a very common mistake. Mr Circumspex, or any other partner in a similar sentence, has been named so it is assumed that he is somehow in a subjective position. But if Mr Circumspex were not a party to the affair, you would find it natural to say 'The doorman allowed me to leave'. The doorman is the subject of that sentence and you are the object of whatever he may grudgingly allow. Even when Mr Circumspex, or any Tom, Dick or Harry, is added, it makes no difference to the fact that **me** is the right pronoun.

Finding the subject can be harder when the sentence is turned about:

> You, Miss Primula and I, Mr
> Circumspex treats well, though he
> kicks his dog.

Even though they come at the beginning of the statement, Miss Primula and the others are really no more than the objects of Mr Circumspex's discrimination. Because 'you' serves as both subjective and objective, should not blind you to the existence of the first person singular objective, 'me'. However Mr Circumspex treats 'me', cavalierly, kindly or rudely. I get the treatment, I do not dish it out. That makes 'me' the object of the sentence. The way to check the validity of a pronoun used in a multiple subject or object is to substitute one word representing the pronoun for the group of words.

> We, Mr Circumspex treats well

looks as bad as it is; commonsense dictates that it should be

> Us, Mr Circumspex treats well

The Raw Materials

or even more plainly,

> Mr Circumspex treats us well

rather than

> Mr Circumspex treats we well.

If any disentanglement shows the statement to be nonsense, you find the right word.

Other people get mishandled as well; grammatical mistakes are not confined to the first and second person:

> It was her that made the mistake,
> they told Miss Primula.

'They', in this instance, are not only un-diplomatic but also grammatically unsound. There are two statements in the sentence:

> They told Miss Primula

and

> (she) made the mistake.

'It was' is simply introductory window-dressing. Separated out, you can see that Miss Primula, bless her, is the subject of the statement 'made the mistake' in spite of her inefficiency.

Relative pronouns are not concerned with number.

> The man who broke the bank at Monte
> Carlo

has the same relative pronoun as

> The subscribers who complain about
> telephone bills.

The Raw Materials

They are nevertheless concerned with case. The case of the pronoun used not only identifies but also particularizes the antecedent, whether it is the subject or object of the sentence.

In

> Miss Primula, who is Mr
> Circumspex'a secretary, goes
> shopping in her lunch hour,

we have two statements:

> Miss Primula goes shopping

and

> Miss Primula is Mr Circumspex's
> secretary.

This sentence concentrated attention on her shopping habits but made it quite clear that we knew which Miss Primula, from any assortment of similarly-named females (she may have sisters - the Misses Primula), chooses to shop at lunchtime. Relative clauses introduce a second element into a statement; the use of the relative pronoun shows that it is an identifying or defining element. You will find more about defining and non-defining clauses in Chapter Five, under **Commas.** We can see how the relative clause works if we reverse the sentence

> Miss Primula, who goes shopping in
> her lunch hour, is Mr Circumspex's
> secretary.

Her occupation is now more important than her habits.

'Whom' gives people much more trouble than the subjective pronoun. To understand its uses, we must be clear about the distinction between the

object and the indirect object. English has developed, over a number of centuries, into a language capable of expressing complex thoughts and ideas. A variety of expressive techniques and devices have evolved so that the speaker or writer is not forced to use a great number of simple statements, in the manner of a child's primer.

> I go walking;
> I go walking many times;
> I walk with my friend;
> My friend is called Miss Primula.

It is so much simpler to say

> I often go walking with my friend,
> Miss Primula.

In a statement like 'Miss Primula gave him the letter' it may seem as if the object is 'him'. If the sentence is taken apart - 'Miss Primula gave the letters' and 'she gave the letters to him' - we see that the 'letters' are what was given and must be the object. But they were given 'to him' and that is the indirect object. The **dative case** represents the object indirectly governed by the verb; the person **to whom** or **for whom** the action takes place. There is no separate case-form for the dative. The objective case-form has to serve.

If it is remembered that 'whom' is properly used for the object of a sentence or clause, we must also be careful to use it for the indirect object. Again, separation and substitution will help to find the necessary case.

> Mr Circumspex, whom we know

is correct because it can be expressed as

> we know him.

The Raw Materials

If the phrase had been

>   Mr Circumspex, who we know,

we would be forced, in substituting the matching pronoun, to say

>   we know he,

recognizable as instant nonsense.

Because written English must be clearer and less ambiguous than speech, it is worth taking trouble over phrasing. Make a practice of stating things so that the pronoun for the indirect object is given the appropriate preposition:

>   he is the man to whom the letters
>   were given

and

>   tell me for whom the letters are
>   intended.

Both are better than their alternatives:

>   he is the man whom the letters were
>   given to

and

>   tell me whom the letters are
>   intended for.

That sort of bad phrasing leads to the mistaken use of the subjective 'who' because the sentences sound awkward. A common, and perfectly proper, idiomatic usage helps to cause confusion between 'who' and 'whom'. We say

The Raw Materials

I know he has it

and therefore we can also say

tell me who has it.

Both 'he' and 'who' are correctly subjective because they are the subjects of **relative clauses**. We shall look at the relative pronoun in detail next but, for the sake of a clear understanding of 'who' and 'whom', look at the two sentences again. Examine the function of the word 'who' and see where, in the first sentence, a word has been left out, or skipped over. Idiomatic usage allows us to phrase such statements leaving the word 'that' to be understood by the hearer or reader. The subjective nature of 'he' and 'who' in these examples is plain if we say

I know that he has it,

and if we know that 'who' is a relative pronoun introducing the clause

who has it,

a statement in its own right.

The most important function of a relative pronoun is that it joins two statements together. It 'conjoins', or acts as a conjunction.

There were once some people called
Sioux
Who spent all their time making
shioux
Which they coloured in various
hioux ...

The Raw Materials

There are three statements here, usefully joined by relative pronouns:

    There were people called Sioux;
    they spent their time making shoes;
    the shoes were made in various
    colours.

The relative pronouns "who" and "which" obviously differentiate between the "people" making things and the "things" they made. It would also have been possible to use "that" in either case. Plainly there are a number of pronouns, some of which can be used in a more general way.

To clarify their use, we can classify the relative pronouns. The personal pronouns can only have **persons** as antecedents. The neuter pronoun is only used when referring to a **thing.** But **that** may refer to either persons or things. There is no differ-ence between singular and plural uses.

	Personal	Neuter	Personal & neuter
Subjective	Who	Which	That
Objective	Whom	Which	That
Indirect	To,for,at		
Object	Whom	Which	
Possessive	Whose	Of which	
	Whose		

"That" may sound the most useful of pronouns, but there are certain restrictions on its use. We can say

    The secretary that types Mr.
    Crcumspex's letters is on holiday

because it implies that there are several secretaries, one of whom is on holiday. But it would be inappropriate to say

> Mrs Circumspex that is staying in
> London is on a shopping trip.

Mr Circumspex, with all his faults, is not, as far as we know, married to more than one woman at a time. The proper relative pronoun must be 'who', not 'that'. 'That' cannot be preceded by a **preposition.** We may not say

> the car in that Mr Circumspex
> drives

although we may say

> the car in which Mr Circumspex
> drives.

If 'that' is used, the preposition must be slotted in later:

> the car that Mr Circumspex drives
> in.

So

> in which I trust

becomes, with a change to 'that'

> that I trust in.

English is a very elastic language. Although a distinction has been made between the personal and neuter pronouns, there are times when we apply the personal pronouns to non-persons. A neuter, or impersonal, pronoun seems right when we say

> the cat which Mr Circumspex kicked
> was a stray animal.

The Raw Materials

It was also an anonymous animal and one hardly valued by the outrageous Mr Circumspex. On the other hand, animals and objects regarded fondly and treated as near-human are often given a personal pronoun:

> my teddybear Rambo, who shares my
> pillow

or

> Hepsibah, our cat, who was kicked
> by Mr Circumspex.

There is also an elegant convention observed in using 'which', 'of which' and 'whose'.

> The houses which have red roof
> tiles are clumped together

can become, if we use the possessive, either

> the houses whose roof tiles are red

or

> the houses, the roof tiles of which
> are red.

The first two sentences say the same thing: those houses which have red roof tiles are in some way segregated from other houses which do not have red roof tiles. But notice that the last statement about tiles is set off from the rest of the sentence with a comma. It is plain to us that all the houses referred to have red tiles. Be careful that the form you choose reflects just what you mean to say. There will be more to say about relative clauses later, and the use of commas will be found in the chapter on punctuation.

Demonstrative pronouns demonstrate. They are used to indicate or point out things or people:

The Raw Materials

This is my house and that is Miss Primula's.

There is also an indication of position; a thing or things nearer to you will get 'this' and 'these'; objects further away are given 'that' and 'those'. Take care that you attach the demonstrative pronoun to the right word. In colloquial speech, the sloppy constructions 'these kind of' or 'those sort of' are often heard. They must never occur in written work. 'These' and 'those' are plural forms and may not be attached to a singular noun. 'This kind of' or 'these kinds of' are the only acceptable constructions. Stick to "this kind of cake" and "these sorts of events".

If a proper pronoun is one that is substituted for a noun or pronoun, then 'this' and 'that', 'these' and 'those' do not always behave like true pronouns. Sometimes they are attached to nouns and act descriptively.

This customer ate five cakes but
will pay for four.

A wise waitress does not want to accuse the wrong person of either greed or fraud, so she uses 'this' to specify or describe the culprit. In that instance 'this' is an adjective qualifying 'customer'. That sentence, and this one, contains more examples of the same construction. But in the sentence

Mr Circumspex said it was not a

kick; that was more a push with his
foot

'that' is used as as a **demonstrative pronoun.**

The Raw Materials

This distinction between pronoun-use and adjectival-use can also be applied to possessive pronouns. It is often argued that 'my book' consists of an adjective describing the noun 'book', and that 'my' is a personal adjective rather than a pronoun. As the purpose of this book is to clarify misunderstandings and help to eliminate misusage, the fine points of classification are left to the reader. If your reason for using the book is the improvement of your standard of written English usage, there is little need to waste intellectual energy on examining the nomenclature if you understand the principles. What you must be certain about is the difference between 'her' used as an object or indirect object and 'her' in the possessive sense. You must be equally certain about the proper use of 'I' and 'me', 'we' and 'us', and 'he' and 'him'. If you identify the noun that is the antecedent for the pronoun as the subject or object of the statement, no matter how twisted about the statement may have become, then you should always be able to choose the right pronoun.

The **interrogative pronouns** give little trouble. 'Who' and 'whose' apply to persons and the same word serves for singular and plural uses, for example:

> Who is Mr Circumspex?

and

> Whose umbrella was left behind?

For inanimate objects, the pronoun is 'which':

> Which house is Miss Primula's?

turns into

> Which is Miss Primula's house?

The Raw Materials

Indefinite pronouns sound vaguer than they are.
While we might shout

> Won't anyone help?

without knowing who might turn up, if we say

> the Circumspexes have two children;
> both are ugly and one is
> badtempered,

you may feel that we are being pretty definite
about the Circumspex children. Nevertheless,
'both' and 'anybody', like 'one', are indefinite
pronouns, and so are 'all', 'someone', 'somebody',
'nobody', 'none' and 'no one'. They do not change
for the subjective or objective cases but a few
have a possessive case:

> I have eaten my doughnut, but that
> one is no one's,

which is not elegantly expressed but allows you to
scoff the last doughnut with a clear conscience.

The **negative pronouns** are bound up with the indefinite pronouns and what are called **distributive**
pronouns, the group comprising 'each', 'every',
'either', 'other' and 'another'. 'Each other'
expresses an exchange or reciprocity of action
between two people or things:

> They complement each other.

'One another' was formerly used where more than
two persons or agents were involved:

> I command you to love one another

but it is often found today as a substitute for

The Raw Materials

'each other'.

Negative pronouns are simply the negative forms of some indefinite and distributive pronouns. Familiar as they are, it is worth mentioning them: 'none', 'nobody', 'no one', 'neither'. 'Neither', like 'either', will appear later in another context. Already you will have seen that some of the words described as pronouns can also be adjectives. English is an economical language and a number of words fulfil more than one purpose. If, however, the writer is not himself sure of the sense in which the words have been used, the reader is unlikely to interpret for him.

Distinguishing Marks - Adjectives

Adjectives bring the world about us to life. They colour the things we see and know about so that we can separate a person or object from the other persons or objects about: a 'red' geranium, 'dingy' curtains, a 'wicker' chair, the 'broken' bicycle. They **qualify** nouns, which have a general application, by making them particular; qualifying gives a more complete picture, attributing qualities and describing condition.

Adjectives distinguish between objects of the same sort: a 'clearing' bank and a 'merchant' bank, and between objects which share the same word but not the same meaning: 'a muddy bank', and 'the Dogger Bank'. They can also be used to show our personal view or opinion of people, events or things:

'nasty' bats and 'nice' rats;
a 'good' party and my 'unhappy' life;
I am 'unbending' but you are 'stiff-necked';
Mrs Circumspex is 'prejudiced' because Miss

The Raw Materials

Primula is 'bigoted' - even Mr Circumspex,
who, although he is 'unprincipled', feels
'superior' when he finds that his partner is
'dishonest'.

More than one adjective can be applied to the same
noun:

'pretty, young' girl
or
'broken-down, old car'

But both still qualify the noun. The word **qualify**
tells us that the noun has been singled out and
its characteristics drawn to our attention.
Qualification does not stop at one or two words. A
whole phrase or class can be used to particularize
something further: the singer 'who sat in a
duckpond of dirty water'. It may be described as
an **adjectival phrase** or a **relative clause,** but it
has the same function as the single word. Pronouns
can become adjectives, as we have already seen;
some nouns and parts of verbs also find themselves
acting as adjectives:

a 'walnut' tree, a 'running' dog.

So far, so good. The comparative form of adjectives need closer attention. **Comparatives** give
us degrees or measures of quality:

I am proud of my 'hairy old' pig but my
neighbour says that he has a pig which is
'hairier' and 'older'. He claims that his
pig is the 'hairiest, oldest' pig in
Wiltshire.

My hairy pig is positive, the rival hairy pig uses
a comparative and my neighbour has gone for the
superlative in his outrageous claim to have the

The Raw Materials

hairiest pig.

If a man descends into gluttony, he becomes
greedy, greedier, greediest. But if his appearance
undergoes, in the same progression, a startling
improvement he cannot become beautiful,
beautifuller, beautifullest. Instead he has to add
one of the irregular comparatives, 'more' and
'most' or use another word with its own
comparative forms, like 'handsome'. Here are the
most usual comparatives classed as irregular:

Positive	Comparative	Superlative
Good	Better	Best
Bad	Worse	Worst
Many	More	Most
Much	More	Most
Little	Less	Least
Hind	(Hinder)	Hindmost
Fore		Foremost

Notice that two words 'many' and 'much' have the
same comparative and superlative forms. They are
not, under any circumstances, to be regarded as
interchangeable for that reason. 'Many' is an
adjective of number and 'much' is an adjective of
quantity. Two other adjectives are frequently
abused by careless substitution: 'less' and
'fewer'. 'Less' is once again a measure of
quantity and 'fewer' can refer only to number. To
say (as many ignorantly do) that there will be
'less' apples on our trees is incorrect.

> We have had 'less' sunshine, 'fewer'
> sunny days, so the crop will be 'less',
> with 'fewer' apples.

In written work it is always better to use 'small'
to indicate size, and keep 'little' to show
quantity.

The Raw Materials

Carelessness sometimes overdoes things and the comparatives 'more', 'most', 'less', 'least' find themselves added to a form that is already comparative, or even added instead of the word's own comparative form:

> adding sugar made the cake 'more sweeter';
> he is 'less poor' than Mr Circumspex.

Avoid such careless mistakes. There is a case, however, to be put for occasionally using 'more' and 'less' with the simple form of the adjective when it advances the meaning more clearly:

> I find I am 'less poor' than I was yesterday:
>
> events proved him to be even 'more wise' than we had thought.

3 SEEING SOME ACTION

Verbs - Words to Make the Wheels Go Round

If we use a noun to name something and adjectives to describe that something in particular, how do we know what happens to the something? It is all very well knowing that there are wolves, one of which is big and bad, and pigs, one of which is pretty, pink and plump, but we need to know more. What have they to do with each other? What is their relationship? It is the interaction that is really interesting. Things begin to look up when we learn that the big bad wolf ate the pretty pink plump pig, or that the pig was eaten by the wolf. However, it is not the destiny of all wolves to eat pigs or for pigs to see their future as pork chops for wolves. The pig might escape, or eat the wolf.

Verbs, then, show what action took place, is taking place or will take place. One must not confuse action, in this sense, and activity. If the subject is thinking, sitting or just lying about, the verb tells us that something is happening. Even a statement like "nothing happened" expresses negative activity.

English verbs can describe a great variety of actions. Each verb has a number of different forms which can be used to show the type of action, the

Seeing Some Action

time of action, the number of persons or things involved, the person or thing that is acting or acted upon and whether or not the action is carried over from one person or thing to another. Some forms act as nouns or adjectives. This abundance means that we must choose the right verb in the right form to convey meaning from all the verbs on offer and all the possible forms. Choice becomes much easier if the forms and their functions are understood.

Verbs have two main functions and these are distinguished by whether the action is limited or not. All verbs make assertions about either action or state. The **finite** forms of the verb are limited by number, person and time. A simple statement like

　he blew his nose

illustrates this. The limitations of

number:
　　　only one nose-blower;
person:
　　　he blew, not you or I, and
time:
　　　he blew, not blows,

are quite clear. On the other hand, the same verb is at work in

　　blowing your nose too hard can
　　damage your ears,

but it is only the idea of action. In the same way you can say

　　I don't like to hear people blowing
　　their noses

and yet the word 'blowing' could mean one person

or fifty, today or yesterday; it is **infinite** because the action is not restricted by the same
limitations that affect the finite form.

For the sake of convenience the principal parts of
the verb are named:

Infinitive: to drive, (to) drive
Present tense: drive
Past tense: drove
Present participle: driving
Past participle: driven

I shall come back to the infinitive later; for the
moment it is enough to say that when we name a
particular verb, we do so as 'to drive' or 'to
be'. The 'to' has no purpose of its own, and
lingers on as a reminder of the ancient roots of
the language and in certain constructions. But it
is present in the name of the verb. The parts of
the verb that first engage attention are those
that directly describe action or state: the finite
forms.

Although the finite forms of the verb are limited
by person, number and time, they are not proof
against the careless user. Human error can make
nonsense of them. As we know, every sentence has a
subject, a noun or pronoun, stated or implied. The
human operator, the writer, must match the subject
to the verb. It is not the fault of the verb when
a singular subject is teamed with a plural verb
form. The mismatch is entirely the writer's doing.
When a reviewer in "The Times" mentions that

there are the usual plethora of misprints
and avoidable editorial errors,

he has committed a grammatical naughtiness.
'Plethora' is singular, no matter how many
misprints and other horrors it embraces, and

Seeing Some Action

deserves a singular verb, 'is'. But this would have made the sentence just as bad. If he wanted to use the word 'plethora', the sentence would have to be recast as

the usual plethora of misprints is there.

Jolly as it is to use a whapdoodle word like 'plethora"', it would have made a better English sentence to abandon it and write

misprints and avoidable editorial errors are abundant.

The advertising copywriter responsible for the poster, shown on London buses, carrying the slogan 'Graffiti is vandalism' needs a dictionary. 'Graffiti' is the plural form of the noun "'graffito', drawing or writing scratched on a wall. The fact that only the plural form is used in current English does not make it singular. If you want to use the word, respect its plural nature.

Remember that the pronoun which is the subject can lead one astray.

'No one of Johannes's trios have moved me more' said Clara Schumann,

stretching artistic licence to breaking point by ignoring the inescapable fact that only one of Brahms's trios was the subject. One is one and ever more shall be so. When the sentence is about one of a number of things, that one is singular.

Compound subjects take a plural verb:

Verbosity and pomposity are the weapons of the bore.

Seeing Some Action

Plural pronouns take a plural verb:

>   They say that love is blind.

Obviously, the verb agrees with the subject, and it is the writer's job to see to that agreement. But when the compound subject consists of first and second person pronouns joined by a third person, the verb must agree with the first or second person, not the third;

>   You and I and Mr Circumspex ride in the
>   first car

will be just as valid when the proper noun is replaced by a pronoun:

>   You and I and he ride in the first car.

Take care when you are using collective nouns or nouns of multitude. When you have chosen to refer to the crowd collectively, you must continue to use a singular verb:

>   the crowd is growing restless.

If you treat it from the beginning as a noun of multitude, stay plural:

>   the crowd are getting out of control

You must never treat the County Council as a group one minute and a number of individuals the next. Consistency is the order of the day.

The finite, or limited forms of the verb "to drive" are the

present tense, "drive",
past tense, "drove".

Seeing Some Action

Singular

```
1st person:    I drive;  I drove
2nd person:    You drive; (you) drive; you drove
3rd person:    He, she it drives; he, she it drove
```

Plural

```
1st person:    We drive;    we drove
2nd person:    You drive;    you drove
3rd person:    They drive;   they drove
```

You can see that the noun or pronoun in front of
the verb, or associated with it, determines the
person of the verb. Even when the testy passenger
says to the chatty taxi-driver 'Drive!', he is
really saying 'You drive!' and using the second
person.

In verbs which behave in a neat and predictable
way, the only change that is likely to occur is in
the third person singular. As we have seen, the
fact that the subject is in the third person
singular may be overlooked if there is a phrase or
clause between the subject and the verb. Mr
Circumspex's habit of mumbling, like the untidy
files, overflowing wastebaskets and dirty windows,
drives Miss Primula to distraction. As Mr C. has
only one habit of mumbling, the verb used could
not have been 'drive'.

To satisfy the relationship of time to action, a
verb is divided into tenses, each representing the
timing of the action. The tense sequence also
indicates whether an action is complete or
continuing and can express past intention which
may or may not have been carried out. The perfect
tenses relate an event or action which has been
completed at the time of the tense used.

Seeing Some Action

Here they are set out for you to note

Present:	I drive
Continuous:	I am driving
Present perfect:	I have driven
Continuous:	I have been driving
Past:	I drove
Continuous:	I was driving
Past perfect:	I had driven
Continuous:	I had been driving
Future	I shall drive
Continuous:	I shall be driving
Future perfect:	I shall have driven
Continuous:	I shall have been driving

There is a further tense which can cause some headaches. It shows that action was expected or stated to be about to take place in the past. It is described as Future-in-the-past.

Future-in-the-past:	(I said that) I would drive
Continuous	(I thought) I would be driving
Future-perfect-in-the-past	(I knew) I should have driven
Continuous	(I expect) I should have been driving

You will notice that all tenses other than the simple present and past add another verb for complete expression. These are the **auxiliary verbs** 'to be' and 'to have', 'shall' and 'will', 'should' and 'would', with the addition, in some

50

cases, of 'do', 'may' and 'might'. 'Do' and 'did' are used to ask questions:

Did you drive?

They are also used for emphasis:

I do drive,

and for negation:

I did not drive.

'May' and 'might' convey possibility or probability, but not certainty:

I may drive

or

I might have driven.

Some verbs used as auxiliaries are verbs in their own right. The reason we take a close look at tenses is the possibility of confusing the use of a verb as auxiliary with its use as the principal verb in a sentence. If you say

I need to drive,

'need' is the principal verb and 'to drive' is the infinitive, acting as the object of the statement. If you replace 'need' in that sentence with 'can', 'ought', 'must' or 'dare', although the 'to' is lost after 'can' and "'must', the situation is the same. 'Drive' or 'to drive' must be the object of the statement.

A peculiarity of the verb 'to be' is that it acts like an equals sign; the word on either side of it is in the subjective case.

Seeing Some Action

Mr Circumspex is her employer

can be instantly reversed with exactly the same meaning:

Her employer is Mr Circumspex.

'Mr Circumspex' and 'her employer' are one and the same. The uneasy area of use is the choice of following pronouns in the simple statements 'it's me' and 'it's him'. The first thing to be established is the use of the apostrophe in 'it's'. If you look at the possessive pronouns in Chapter Two, you will see that the third person neuter pronoun has no apostrophe. It does not need one because the 's' belongs to the word just as it does in 'his' or 'hers'. If you have ever been guilty of writing 'her's', don't do it again. And if you always play safe and give the possessive 'its' an apostrophe, stop it at once.

The apostrophe only appears in 'it's' when it is a shortened verb form, representing 'it is' or 'it has'. It has no possessive meaning. Because 'it's me' is an abbreviation of 'it is me', using the verb 'to be', the notion has been put about that it is a grammatical error and that correct usage favours 'it is I'. It is a silly notion. Prepare to defend yourself if attacked. The French, who guard the purity of their language with vigour, use a similar construction and regard it as correct; a simple statement, 'il est malade', uses the ordinary subjective case, 'he is ill', but uses an emphatic nominative in 'c'est moi' (it is me) or 'c'est lui' (it's him). The fact that there is an exact parallel in a language that has, during the Norman domination, influenced English, gives 'it's me' a healthy and respectable aspect. Nevertheless, the wayward nature of the language does not allow us to use this construction in written English and get away with it.

Seeing Some Action

    It is me who has the responsibility

is just plain bad grammar. And the reason for   it
being   so   is   that   it makes a clumsy and awkward
sentence. It is clearer and more direct to say

    I have the responsibility.

Only say so of course if it is true.

The misplaced apostrophe in 'its' is such a common
mistake that a little more attention may help   to
make   the   distinction   clearer.   In the following
sentence 'it is' can   always   be   substituted   for
'it's'. All instances properly take an apostrophe:

    It's interesting;
    It's a bad day for cats;
    It's a cat, not a dog;
    It's mine.

In the next set of examples, 'its' is a possessive
pronoun and must never have an apostrophe:

    Its fur stood on end;
    The cat went through its cat door;
    The upside-down umbrella exposes its
    spokes;
    Its intention is to protect.

Transition and Voice - the Receiving End

Verbs are described as **transitive** or **intransitive**
A transitive verb is one through which the action
is   passed   from   the   subject   to   an object. The
action of an intransitive verb is complete in
itself:

    Rain fell; Miss Primula languished.

Seeing Some Action

Even when another word appears to follow an intransitive verb, as in 'she fell down', 'fall' remains an intransitive verb because 'down' is an **adverb modifying the action.** Transitive verbs must have an object to complete the sense, such as 'Baby made mud pies', or 'Miss Primula feeds birds'. Some verbs can change sides and behave either transitively or intransitively:

>Mrs Circumspex rang the bell:
>The telephone rang.

To complicate matters, intransitive verbs are sometimes followed by a noun that has a meaning related to the verb. This is a **cognate** (or understood) **object**:

>Mr Cirumspex lived a double life.

Sometimes the noun is a little more distantly related:

>She played a good game.

Sometimes the cognate noun is left out but its meaning lingers on:

>Miss Primula played Lady Macbeth.

Of course, we all know that she played 'the part of Lady Macbeth'. At times only the adjective qualifying the cognate noun is left:

>Mr Circumspex laughed his loudest,

in fact laughing his loudest 'laugh'. And the neuter pronoun can replace the cognate noun:

>The cats fought it out,

Seeing Some Action

fighting the fight out as cats will. Finally a few intransitive verbs can be used as **causatives,** when something or someone causes the action to take place:

>   Water boils,

but

>   Mrs Circumspex boils the water.

The reason for making these distinctions in the nature of words objectively associated with transitive and intransitive verbs lies in the need to be able to understand the function of the words used in the construction of a sentence. If you do not understand the behaviour of the words you use, you will not be able to judge whether you have made them behave as they should. In

>   water boils fiercely,

'fiercely' is an adverb modifying 'boils'. When Me Circumspex says to Miss Primula 'Type me this letter', he is asking her something which can be analysed to show the real relationship of the words:

>   you (the subject) type (transitive verb)
>   a letter (direct object) for me
>   (indirect object).

Life is full of ups and downs. The person or thing on top at one moment may be on the bottom before another minute passes. Sometimes the subject is the doer of the action:

>   Mr Circumspex visited the zoo;
>   an unknown man stole the armadillo.

At other times, the subject is the person or thing to whom or to which the action has been done;

> the zoo was visited by Mr
> Circumspex

and

> the armadillo was stolen by an
> unknown man.

The **active voice** is the verb form used when the subject performs the action. When the sentence or statement is turned about, and the subject is the receiver of the action, the form used is the **passive voice.** If you look at the examples above you will see that in the active voice, each verb is transitive. Generally speaking, only transitive verbs can be used in the passive voice. The simplest example is one where there is no direct or cognate object

> Mr Circumspex prevaricated

which has no room for alteration. The appearance of an indirect object can be confusing. To say

> the chair stood on the Aubusson carpet

makes sense. If we try to turn it about,

> the Aubusson carpet was stood on by
> the chair,

it is recognizably clumsy and the effect is silly. 'Stood' is an intransitive verb modified by an adverbial phrase, 'on the Aubusson carpet'. The carpet is not a direct object. If there is no identifiable object or double object (direct and indirect) a passive construction is impossible. This is an area where mistakes are frequently made and it is important to understand the limitations of intransitive verbs. If the statement had been

> a chair stood in the next room,

Seeing Some Action

the bad grammar resulting from trying to put it into the passive would hit one in the eye:

the next room was stood in by the chair.

It is possible, though seldom justifiable, to make a passive construction with verbs using a cognate object.

The cats fought it out

may be expressed as

it was fought out by the cats,

but only where the 'fight' or 'battle' which is the antecedent for the pronoun 'it' has already been mentioned in the text.

Notice that the passive needs an auxiliary even where the active form does not. For example:

The cat drinks the milk
becomes
the milk is drunk by the cat;

and

the dog is chasing the elephant
becomes
the elephant is being chased by the dog.

The camel kicked the bucket

becomes in the literal sense

the bucket was kicked by the camel.

In every tense, an auxiliary or another auxiliary

has to be added in the passive voice. Furthermore, if you look at these statements again you will see that the passive is always made up of the auxiliary added to the past participle. The past participle, like the infinitive, is one of the 'infinite' parts of the verb. As such it behaves neutrally, incapable of indicating person, number or time. The task of showing time is left to the auxiliary.

The passive voice is used to place the reader's attention on a particular noun or pronoun in the sentence. To the zoo keeper, the elephant is of first importance. He worries about the fact that it is being chased by anything rather than the nature of its enemy. He would still be more concerned about the elephant if it were being chased by a tentpole. It can, then, be used to place emphasis and to give greater importance to the recipient of the action. This is useful in formal statements. 'The Water Board asked me to make a statement' does not define your standing. You will certainly seem rather more of an individual and less of a dogsbody if you phrase it as 'I have been asked by the Water Board to make a statement'. When the Mayor is giving a civic reception for Yogi Bear, we understand that the busy old Mayor is at it again, putting on one of his twice-weekly re- ceptions for some bear or other. To raise this reception from the obscurity of clouds of entertainment, we can concentrate on the guest.

> Yogi Bear is being given a civic
> reception by the Mayor.

Your attention is drawn to the recipient and this will enable you to choose to applaud his elevation or decide that the Mayor should be removed from office. The passive is used effectively in advertising: 'you have been chosen' and 'you will

Seeing Some Action

be pleased by' something rather than 'we have chosen you' and 'it will please you'.

Manner and Time

The verb combinations which make up the tenses allow us to indicate a wide variety of times in which events take place. Custom dictates, however, that we shall not invent combinations to suit our convenience but that we shall use those which are regarded as indicating time most precisely. Moreover, we should avoid confusing the reader by mixing tenses improperly. The time shown in one part of the sentence should relate to that shown in any other part of the same sentence unless there is an intended change of time to be shown:

     I woke up when the sun rose
but
     I told him you would be waiting.

The only time when one is able to join a statement in the present to one in the past is when a universal truth is being stated, or the sub-ordinate statement deals with an ongoing situation while the main statement is in the past:

     they told me that the scar is
     permanent.

Verbs, however, are expected to convey more than the numbers acting and the time of action. They also show the manner of action, called the **mood**. The **indicative mood** is very straightforward. It asserts facts and matters of fact:

     cream is fattening;
     the camel escaped his keeper;
     the cat has eaten Mr Circumspex's
     lamb chop.

Seeing Some Action

The **imperative mood** is one of command and instruction:

> Go home;
> drive with care;
> take a letter;
> stir the egg whites into the cream.

Even when it is softened with a polite or placating word, it is still in the imperative mood:

> Please take a letter, Miss Primula.

Where the indicative mood deals with facts and the imperative mood makes firm statements, the **subjunctive mood** is one of possibility and uncertainty. The subjunctive mood supposes that anything may happen, may be happening or may have happened, but does not admit the supposition to be fact:

> If I were as powerful as you say;
> were you to attend the meeting;
> if he should wish to buy.

These are all subjunctive clauses, which are usually preceded by 'if'. The subjunctive could be described as the mood of hypothesis or possibility:

> if the house fell down, I could
> live in the garden hut.

In that example, 'fell down' could be replaced by 'were to fall down'. This is the test of a subjunctive: if the subjunctive mood of the verb 'to be' can be substituted for the verb form used, and the sense is the same, then it is a sub-junctive and not a conditional clause. I shall

Seeing Some Action

come to conditional clauses in a moment, but first let us look at the subjunctive of the verb 'to be'.

Present singular: I be, you be, he,she,it be;
Present plural: we be, you be, they be:

Past singular: I were, you were, he,she,it were;
Past plural: we were, you were, they were.

Most of the present tense forms have disappeared from English usage. Rather than 'if you be the man you claim to be', we say 'if you are the man ...' in modern English. But no one can fail to understand 'Be it ever so humble, there's no place like home'. The past forms, however, are in current use as auxiliaries and give the flavour of something that might happen in circumstances good or bad. It is a wish or fear expressed but not the whole statement in most cases. When we say 'God save the Queen', we are not ordering God to do a task; instead we ask that the Queen **may be saved.** Although some modern grammarians regard the subjunctive as a leftover mood, rarely used, it has a place in good written English that is both useful and justifiable. It is a usage better recognized in American English, though it is almost as widely used in Britain.

Not just a literary device, it has a role in business correspondence:

you could see the equipment in action if you were to visit the factory:

if we were to meet for lunch the matter could be discussed informally:

the staff would be upset if he were to be reinstated.

This is language that is both formal and simple. We recognize the need for a formal attitude in certain circumstances and it is a pity that too often the desire to be formal and impersonal leads people to compose overloaded and complicated sentences to achieve it. Simplicity is the sign of a well-used subjunctive. It is also of value in refuting arguments, by exposing the hypothetical nature of objection or criticism:

if your claim were true, the battle would have been over after two days, not five;

The conditional clause is used where one action depends on another:

If you pull the cat's tail, she will scratch you:

If you have finished that drink, I'll buy you another.

All conditional clauses of this sort are in the indicative mood, not the subjunctive, so you will notice that there is a different tense sequence. The present, present continuous or present perfect tense may be followed by a future tense.

If you are still working

is a statement set in the present;

I will leave the light on

has not yet occurred.

Seeing Some Action

One can get away with a careless misusage in colloquial speech - one's facial expression and an explanatory phrase can clear up mis-understandings. But when the reader must take what you say at face value, it is well to distinguish between the subjunctive if-clause with its sense of what is wished for or feared and the conditional if-clause which makes one action positively depend on another action.

Infinite Forms: The Flexible Verb

The three infinite and unrestricted forms of the verb are the **infinitive** and the **present** and **past participles.** Before we look at them more closely, remember that we have already seen them at work in forming tenses with auxiliaries. When they were used in tense formation, the present and past participles always stayed unchanged and did not themselves give us the time of the action, whether present or future, past perfect or future-in-the-past. The auxiliaries were left to show when an action was occurring or had occurred. Although we form these tenses quite naturally when we speak, it is useful to bear in mind the compounds we use to make them. Because the participles have other functions, it is easy to overlook the fact that they may be performing as part of a finite form.

The first function of the infinitive is to name the verb: 'to be'; 'to howl'; 'to drive'; 'to do'; 'to undo'. When the principal parts of the verb were listed, I mentioned the fact that 'to' is a mere addition to the infinitive and that it is left out in a number of cases. Unfortunately, the 'to' has been responsible for some unnecessary fears.

You may have been told that you must never split

Seeing Some Action

an infinitive. This silly misdirection has left many people feeling that they may do anything but split an infinitive. Infinitive-splitters are so low that conductors refuse their fares and throw them off buses. That is naughty nonsense, particularly so when people have not been taught any grammar and do not know an infinitive even when it plucks at their ankles. When they see the word 'to' in a sentence, they break out in spots though the innocuous preposition has done no harm. They peer nervously at all verbal constructions, fearing that by chance an infinitive may have been split and the world will sneer.

What is this bugbear, the infinitive? As an infinite form of the verb its action is not limited by time, number or person. When I say of Mr Circumspex that 'he walked to his office', the finite form 'walked', refers to one person (number), the second person singular is the subject and it happened in the past (time). On the other hand, if I say of Mr C. that 'he liked to walk to the office', 'to walk' is an infinitive form, saying nothing about who liked to walk, how many liked to walk or when they liked to walk. It remains unaffected by number even when Mr Circumspex is joined by Miss Primula , Mrs Circumspex, Daphne, the office cleaner and her friend Eff; they all like 'to walk'. If 'nobody' likes 'to walk', the infinitive soldiers on, unchanged.

How can this innocuous thing be split? 'Splitting' occurs when an adverb pushes its way between the word 'to' and the rest of the infinitive. Adverbs are descriptive words which do for verbs what adjectives do for nouns; they modify or qualify the action:

He runs slowly.

Seeing Some Action

They are useful because they tell us just how an action was performed. When Mr Circumspex decided 'to meanly stop' his wife's housekeeping money, the infinitive 'to stop' was 'split' by 'meanly'. In order to emphasize the man's niggardliness, an adverb is needed. However, in this instance, nothing has been gained by shoving it into the infinitive. The meaning would be better shown if he 'meanly decided' to stop the money. The adverb must always be placed where it will do the most good.

You should never go out of your way to split an infinitive, even to declare your independence. In most cases it produces an awkward, clumsy sentence. It can also be confusing and usually weakens the statement. But there are times when, for the sake of emphasis, you may put your adverb in the middle. Getting Mr Circumspex 'to firmly deny' that he is a skinflint is stronger than if he were 'to deny it firmly'.

The Shorter Oxford English Dictionary defines the infinitive as 'that form of a verb which expresses simply the notion of the verb without predicating it of any subject'. In other words, it gives us the idea of the verb without making it act like a verb. Although it is a true part of the verb it can function

as the equivalent of a noun:
    I like <u>to drive</u> (the object of 'like');

as the equivalent of an adverb:
    I came <u>to drive</u> the car;

as the equivalent of an adjective:
    I have a car <u>to drive</u>

Without the handy particle 'to' the infinitive may

be harder to recognize, but it is still an infinitive. Daphne, the office cleaner, told Eff what 'she heard Mr Circumspex say'. 'Say', in that statement, is an infinitive; think of it as 'she heard him to say', which is too much of an archaism to be used in good English today but allows you to identify infinitives. If you 'let someone drive your car', 'drive' is an infinitive as well as a favour. In statements where you might otherwise expect to find 'to', if the infinitive comes after the auxiliary verbs 'shall', 'should', 'can', 'must', 'may', 'might', 'will', 'would', 'do', and 'did', the 'to' is always omitted.

The present participle, as you can see from the table of tenses, is used with an auxiliary to produce the continuous tenses:

> I was driving.

By itself it can be a noun, acting as the subject of a sentence:

> Long-distance driving is very
> boring.

The verb in that sentence is 'is', with one participle, 'driving', as the subject and another "boring", as the object. The present participle turns into an adjective in uses like 'driving rain'.

The participle can lead an adjectival phrase, which will behave in all respects like a single-word adjective:

> Driving to the office. Mr Circumspex
> hummed a little hate-tune.

The participial phrase qualifies a noun: Mr

Seeing Some Action

Circumspex. It could be expessed as

> Mr Circumspex hummed a little hate-tune
> when (or as) he was driving.

The original phrase, 'driving to the office', shows one of the particular uses of the participle, establishing coincidental time of action. The tune was hummed neither before or after the act of driving, but at the same time. The participle is the same, whatever the coincidental time may be or have been:

> I saw him driving his car yesterday,

which joins the time of driving to the time when the subject was seen. That last example illustrates another characteristic of the participle: it can take an object of its own, 'his car'.

Participles, no matter how useful they may be, are also traps for the unwary. The participial adjective phrase must have a noun to qualify but it is all too easy to fail to attach it to the right noun.

> Being in a angry mood, Miss Primula
> dreaded Mr Circumspex's summons.

But poor Miss Primula is frightened, not angry; it is her employer who is cross. The participle, 'being', is wrongly attached. There are two constructions which give rise to a great many errors. If the main clause begins with 'there' and the sentence has been started with an adjectival phrase, the sentence can easily get into trouble:

> Having shouted at everyone, there is
> little chance that Mr Circumspex will
> apologize.

Seeing Some Action

The really horrid and ignorant mistake is to leave
the participle hanging in mid-air. This can happen
with impersonal constructions, where the main
statement begins with 'it':

> Referring to the report in this morning's
> paper, it seems obvious that Mr
> Circumspex was driving too fast.

The only thing that the adjectival phrase can
attach itself to is 'it', making the sentence
nonsense. And there are many pairs of sharp eyes
detecting mistakes of that sort, so the writer
should beware. The participle 'referring' often
gives rise to errors in business correspondence,
where its use in introductory phrases has become
part of boring office jargon:

> Referring to your letter, you may be
> unaware of the extent of your overdraft.

It is the writer who is referring to the letter,
not the overdrawn recipient, but he simply picked
up the piece of gobbledegook and stuck it on the
front of the sentence without thinking. How
galling it must be to owe money to a bank that
allows such ungrammatical letters to be sent.

When the participle is used as a noun, it is often
called a gerund in order to distinguish it from
both ordinary nouns (which have no verbal
character) and adjectival participles. There are
two possible constructions using the gerund:

> Playing poker can make you poor.

or

> The playing of poker can make you poor.

The second construction is not often used today
but it illustrates one of the pitfalls encountered
when making a statement with gerunds. If the

Seeing Some Action

gerund is the subject of the sentence or clause, any noun or pronoun that qualifies it must be in the possessive case. Miss Primula would be wrong to say that 'Mr Circumspex shouting upset her' because it is the man's noise that she dislikes; she must change it to 'Mr Circumspex's shouting upset her'. It is clearer if we use a pronoun instead of the noun: 'His shouting upset her', not 'Him shouting'. So

> The driver taking the wrong route made us late

is often heard in colloquial speech but must, in writing, be changed to

> The taking of the wrong route by the driver

or, better and simpler,

> The driver's taking the wrong route.

The reader must see that 'taking' the wrong route is the subject, but that the person responsible is the 'driver', so the two words are bound together by making the qualifying word possessive.

English idiom requires that some words shall only be followed by a gerund and others shall only take the infinitive. Careful reading of dictionary definitions may help to identify the right usage; it will certainly tell you the right preposition to use. However haste, or perhaps an inability to hear bad constructions, can lead to some inexcusable mistakes. "The Times" has recently printed, not once but several times, sentences in which someone has been forbidden 'from' doing something. A thing can be forbidden:

> Overtaking on the left is forbidden

and you can forbid someone 'to do' something:

> It is forbidden to overtake on the left.

As 'forbid' is a compound word based on 'bid', we
can show how wrong things go with 'from':

> He bids me from doing it.

So idiomatically we 'object to going' somewhere,
but 'refuse to go' there; we 'confess to
committing' crimes, but 'profess to commit' them;
we have a 'habit of giggling', but a 'tendency to
giggle'.

The past participle can be recognized by its
ending: -n, -en, -d or -t. Like the present
participle it can be used as a verbal adjective.
Its character, however, is quite different. Where
the present participle tells us something that is
done or being done by the subject, the past
participle tells us something that has happened to
the subject: a 'falling star' is in the act of
falling, but the 'fallen angel' has lost Paradise.
If we examine a statement like

> The candidate, rejected by the Board,
> left the building,

we can see that the sense is

> The candidate who was rejected by the
> Board.

It is in the passive voice. It is still in the
passive voice when it becomes an adjectival phrase
or clause: The (who-was-rejected) candidate.

The verb 'ejected' is a transitive verb; we cannot
just 'reject', but must always reject something or

somebody. If the participle used is part of a transitive verb, it is never used in the active voice, only the passive. The active and passive voices are easily picked out in the tenses: 'I buy bread' and 'Bread was bought yesterday' show the reversal of the subject from the bread-buyer to the bread. This pattern persists in using the participles.

> After buying this bread yesterday, I
> found that it was mouldy

becomes

> This bread, bought yesterday, was found
> to be mouldy.

The past participle, like the present, needs to be related to the noun it qualifies. If it is not, an ambiguous or confusing statement can appear. In

> The mother of the candidate, rejected by
> the Board, left the building,

the subject of the sentence is 'mother' and we have to assume that it was she whom the Board sent packing. While such a statement can be redeemed by inserting a relative pronoun and an auxiliary verb:

> The mother of the candidate who was
> rejected,

there is still ambiguity and the writer's intention is uncertain. As far as we know, Mother hasn't even seen the Board; it is her son, poor fellow, who has been found unworthy or unsuitable. But did she leave the building alone, or are we meant to take it that they both left after the unhappy incident? Perhaps

> the candidate, rejected by the Board,
> left the building with his mother.

This sort of time-wasting guesswork results from carelessness. The first principle of writing is to leave no doubt in the reader's mind about your meaning.

The change from the active voice to the passive, when we use a past participle instead of a present participle, gives an immutable change of meaning: a 'hanging judge' is a bright and lively man when contrasted with a 'hanged judge'. The 'rejecting Board' is not at all the same thing as the 'rejected Board'. These, however, are transitive verbs. It used to be felt that the past participle of intransitive verbs, when used as simple adjectives, could only precede the word qualified, never follow it. Customs change; if they did not, I should have had to say the "qualified word" in the last sentence. But there are limits of tolerance. The 'dead pigeon' is never a 'pigeon dead', nor can a 'withered flower' be a 'flower withered', except in poetry. And if we want to be precise, to say

> I shall have my desk cleared this
> afternoon

carries the sense of the clearing being done for you. If you are clearing up yourself, it is less confusing to say

> I shall have cleared my desk this
> afternoon,

avoiding the misleading adjectival participle, and using a future perfect tense instead. You could also, if you want to use the participle, say

Seeing Some Action

> I shall have a cleared desk this
> afternoon.

Don't overlook the ideomatic peculiarities of the
language, which can produce very different
meanings from a change of word order. If the adjectival past participles of intransitive verbs
were always forced to precede the nouns they
qualified.

> They heard their names called

would have to become

> They heard themselves called names,

and who knows what might not happen. In general
use, however, remember that although we can see
'the storm breaking', we avoid the 'broken spring'
when we sit on the sofa; we see the 'rainbow
fading away', but worry about the 'faded
curtains'. Unlike the present participle, the past
participle never, as part of the infinite verb,
acts as a noun. In

> Stealing whisky is a crime,

the art of stealing, not the whisky, is the
subject of the sentence and is a noun. But this is
not true of

> This whisky is stolen.

Although 'stolen' comes after the verb 'is', it is
not the object of the verb. If analysed (the
sentence, not the whisky), the statement can be
seen as

> This is stolen whisky,

Seeing Some Action

and the past participle is merely an adjective.

The infinite forms of the verb sound more complicated than they really are. The following examples may help to clarify their use:

Nouns

Infinitive: To see is to believe;
                         I have an apple to eat;
                         He hears you say it;

Present participle

    as verbal noun: The writing of a book is hard
                         work;

        as gerund: Seeing is believing;
                         Writing a book is hard work.

Adjectives

Present participle: Making mud pies, the baby
                         became dirty;

Past participle: Broken promises make me angry.

4 PUTTING THINGS TOGETHER

Mortar Between the Bricks

Despite the essential nature of nouns and verbs as
the basic units of communication, they obviously
cannot be used alone to make complex statements.
Other words must fill in the gaps. If there were
no other words, communication would stick at the
'Me Tarzan, you Jane' level. Using adjectives, we
can describe the noun: Me orphaned, jungle-reared,
uneducated, intelligent, muscular young man Tarzan
(you may fill in Jane's adjectives). Plainly this
is cumbersome, and an incomplete way of communi-
cating facts. After nine words we still do not
know what Tarzan wants to say. Perhaps it is just
'My name is Tarzan'. That is still a very simple
statement and the tale might go faster if he could
say

> Wishing to be as fluent and
> civilized as you are, I realize
> that I must start by learning to
> speak.

Many of the words used in that sentence are
neither nouns nor verbs. Others we have met and
they should, by now, be easily identifiable.
'Wishing' is a participle introducing a subordinate clause; 'learning' is a participle turned
gerund; there are two adjectives, 'fluent' and

Putting Things Together

'civilized', finite verbs 'realize' and 'must start', pronouns 'I' and 'you', and an infinitive, 'to speak'. The action of the other, smaller, words and the way in which they help to convey a number of ideas, must be the next thing to consider. All of the words in the sentence are joined together to tell us what is in Tarzan's mind, not joined at random but fitted together according to a pattern which we recognize as familiar. When we read such a sentence, we never bother to analyse it word by word to take in its meaning; because of its familiarity the meaning comes in chunks, as it were. It is when we come to construct a sentence that we pay attention to the pattern because we need to produce something that the reader can recognize. Before looking at the patterns we use, however, it would be as well to examine the nature of the words not yet encountered in this book.

Modifying, Introducing and Joining — Adverbs, Prepositions and Conjunctions

Just as nouns have adjectives which qualify or describe them, so verbs have adverbs which modify or describe the action. The adjective qualifies the noun by limiting the application of the noun to some one thing or group of things:

    apples;
    red apples;
    a worm-eaten apple;
    the rotten apple;
    juicy red apples.

The adverb limits the verb's application in the same way:

    running;
    running badly;

running badly lately.

Adverbs can modify adjectives and other adverbs as well as verbs:

a fairly good cake;
very sincerely yours;
perfectly well.

Although we can find a definition of 'an adverb' and give examples, so many words function sometimes as adverbs and sometimes as other parts of speech, and adverbs add so many meanings to words and groups of words other than verbs, it is the use or function of the word that decides its adverbial nature. Take 'hard work', a 'hard task' and 'He is working hard' as examples. The first two have the word 'hard' acting as an adjective; the third uses 'hard' as an adverb. But this is not true of every adjective. You can 'work hard' but you can't 'work easy'. You have to put up with working 'easily'. She plays the piano 'really well' but she is wearing 'real pearls'.

The same word can act as an adverb in one instance and as a preposition in another instance. A pre-position is a word that expresses the relationship between a noun or pronoun and another word in the sentence. It is said to **govern** that noun or pro- noun, which is always in the objective case and usually follows the preposition. When Mr Circum- spex puts the hat 'on' his head, and we think it looks ridiculous 'on' him, the preposition 'on' governs 'head' and 'him'. But when Mr Circumspex tells MIss Primula not to lock the office because he is staying 'on', the word 'on' is an adverb modifying the verb 'staying'. If the distinction seems difficult, remember that the preposition must have a noun or pronoun to govern but the adverb always describes

Putting Things Together

the action of the verb.

Adverbs	Prepositions
He drove by	He drove by the house
It jumped up	The mouse ran up the curtain
There are but few aardvarks	They eat no food but ants
He follows after	He ran after the bus

The preposition, whatever you may have been told, can be separated from its noun and arrive at the end of the sentence with impunity. There is but one stipulation when it is so used in writing: the word governed by the preposition is always in the objective case. So it is correct to say

He is the man to whom I gave it,

and to change it to

He is the man whom I gave it to,

but bad Englith to say

He is the man who I gave it to.

If, like many people, you find yourself uneasy with 'whom', you can use the relative pronoun 'that' instead. And this will solve your problem, because it is often omitted:

The man I gave it to

is understood as

The man that I gave it to.

Keep in mind, however, that when you have an alternative, the pronoun governed by a preposition

Putting Things Together

is always 'whom' or 'him', 'me' or 'us'. That familiar but inexcusable solecism 'between you and I', or 'between he and I' can be corrected to 'between you and me', or 'between him and me'. This expression always looks better as 'between us', as in 'there is harmony between us'. I recommend that you avoid the others.

Adverbs and adjectives can work alone or in pairs. Several adjectives can be applied where there is a need to describe something very precisely:

> That handsome short bowlegged man.

And adverbs need not come singly:

> He ran uphill easily

A group of words can also do the work of adjectives and adverbs and can be a phrase - a group of words acting together as the equivalent of an adjective or adverb but without a finite verb:

> The roses, heavy with scent, hung
> from the trellis.

The phrase 'heavy with scent' describes the 'roses' (the-heavy-with-scent roses). We can use an adverbial phrase in the same way:

> Mr Circumspex rages in a flamboyant
> manner,

and there 'in a flamboyant manner' acts, in modifying the verb, as a single adverb would.

A clause is part of a sentence but has a subject and finite verb of its own:

> Mr Circumspex, **who had a nasty**

> **temper,** was a flamboyant character;

> The office, **where Miss Primula did her work,** was inconvenient.

You will see that the first adjective clause, describing Mr Circumspex, is introduced by a relative pronoun, 'who', and the other, describing the office, begins with an adverb of place 'where'. Just as an adverb can modify an adjective - she is a 'fairly' good typist; he is a 'very' competent manager - so an adjective clause can be introduced by an adverb. Notice also that the adjective clause, like an adjective, stays close to the noun it qualifies. If it did not, the reader would be confused by a sentence in which a number of nouns are used, because the qualification attaches itself to the wrong noun. - When the crowd in the office parted to let Mr Circumspex, kicking the wastebasket and berating Daphne, the office cleaner, **who had a nasty temper**, appear, it is no longer Mr Circumspex, but poor old Daphne who is badtempered, no matter how many wastebaskets are kicked. Keep the adjective clause and its noun together.

The adverb clause has more freedom. It can follow the verb it modifies: we distrust Mr Circumspex **because we know him**; or begin the sentence: **when the cat's away**, the mice will play. 'Because' introduces an adverb clause of reason or cause and 'when' gives us the time for mice to kick up their heels.

Adverbs, individually, carry their meaning plainly. The idea of action in the verb is directly affected by its modifier:

> He hobbled **painfully.**

Putting Things Together

meaning. As it is part of a complex sentence, the adverb clause is regarded as subordinate to the main clause, the simple statement: 'I like peaches'. To modify that statement, we can add a second idea: 'when they are ripe', but this clause is subordinate to, or dependent on the main clause. It cannot stand alone and make sense.

Often the main clause is shorter than the subordinate clauses:

> If Mr Circumspex, who is not noted for
> his honesty, is telling the truth, I must
> be wrong.

Although 'I must be wrong' is the main clause, it is the subordinate clauses that give the sentence its larger meaning of something grudgingly conceded. The adverb clause, beginning with 'if', limits the action to a concession. Here are some examples of adverb clauses carrying specific limitations of action:

Time:

> (I will answer your letter) when I have
> seen my solicitor;
>
> After he arrived, (he heard that his
> luggage was lost);
>
> (I have been promoted) since you last
> saw me;
>
> Until you hear from me, (stay at home);

Place:

> (She found the trumpet) where she
> looked for it;
>
> Where the markers stand, (the factory

will be built);

Cause:
    (The butter has gone) because the cat
    has eaten it;

Result:
    (They worked so well) that the job was
    finished on time;

Manner:
    (Insulate the roof), as we have done,
    (to save fuel):

Purpose:
    (He insulated the roof) in order that
    he might save fuel;

Concessions:
    Although we added brass polish, (the
    punch was insipid);

Condition:
    If the roof leaks, (water will get into
    the beer.

Prepositions and adverbs, as I have already said,
overlap. Remember that when you fall "down", your
fall is directed by an adverb, but when the cat
falls 'down the well', it is led to its fate by a
preposition. The prepositional phrase is one that
expresses a relationship of time, place or
possession. And, like the preposition itself, it
is used with a noun or pronoun to express the relationship with some other word in the sentence:

She found the trumpet **under the bed;**

She found the trumpet **in five minutes;**

Putting Things Together

> Her trumpet-playing shows the limits **of her talent.**

A sentence can be simple, complex or compound. The simple statement is obvious. The complex statement is one in which several other concepts are joined to the main clause, by means of adjectival phrases, adverbial phrases, prepositional phrases, adjective clauses and adverb clauses. The compound statement is made up of two statements of equal or nearly equal importance joined by a conjunction. The most familiar conjunction is 'and':

> He played chess and I played hockey.

Conjunctions have their set of conventions. They join together, or conjoin, two words:

> bangers and mash; cats and dogs,

or two statements:

> He fell down and she tumbled after him,

or parts of a complex sentence:

> The judge summed up, the jury retired
> and, while they deliberated, the
> prisoner's wife continued to wait
> patiently.

Four separate actions, following each other in time, are covered in one complex sentence.

Although 'and' is the most used and most familiar conjunction, it is much abused. Conjunctions join together things of equal importance or similar construction. They cannot bind a phrase, without a finite verb, to a clause, with a finite verb, but must always join clause to clause or phrase to

phrase   or   word to word. The usual mistake is one
called 'and-whichery', though   it   might   also   be
called 'but-whichery' or 'and-whosery'. In

> The draft, written in haste, and which
> was not corrected, was sent in error,

a   phrase 'written in haste", has been gummed to a
clause, 'and which   not   corrected',   and   the
result   is confusing as well as unwieldy. Although
the sentence would be improved if the phrase   were
upgraded to a clause, 'which was written in haste'
to   match   'which   was not corrected', it would be
even better if it were shortened:

> The draft, written in haste and not
> corrected, was sent in error.

The   'whiches'   were   not   really   necessary.
Complicated   statements can lead to the commission
of complicated mistakes:

> The charges against Socrates rested on
> his rejection of the established Gods -
> which he was supposed to have supplanted
> by new Gods - and who was said to have
> corrupted the young.

'And who' is trying to join a   clause   apparently
qualifying   Socrates   (the   singular   verb   'was'
acquits the   Gods   of   corruption.)   to   the   main
statement   'the   charges   ...   rested   on   his
rejection'. The writer seems to   have   hoped   that
the   clause   could   be attached to the parenthetic
clause qualifying 'Gods', but it failed,   as   many
afterthoughts   do.   Cobbling up a sentence instead
of rewriting it leads   to   some   inexcusable   mistakes. We can put it right:

> The charges against Socrates, who was
> said to have corrupted the young, rested

on his rejection of the established Gods,
whom he was supposed to have supplanted
by new Gods.

We can improve it further:

Socrates was accused of rejecting the
established Gods, introducing new Gods
and corrupting the young.

The simple conjunctions are 'and' and 'but':

I walk home but he goes by bus;

I have a blue car and a grey donkey.

There is a compound conjunction, 'as well as'. And
there are correlative conjunctions, which operate
in pairs:

both ... and
either ... or
neither ... nor
not only ... but also

The short conjunctions 'or' and 'nor' are often
used without 'either' or 'neither'.

He had to choose between pink elephants
or a sober life.

Be careful with 'nor'. It is a negative in its own
right so it can cancel another negative:

It is **not** well written **nor** grammatically
correct.

'Not' has a negative weight that is sufficient to
cover both 'well written' and 'grammatically
correct', so 'nor' should be replaced by 'or'. But

Putting Things Together

we can use it to negate a second statement which it joins to the main statement:

> He has **not** arrived, **nor** has he told us
> why he has been delayed.

There 'nor' stands for 'and he has not'.

The correlative conjunctions must be used together:

> He is **both** handsome **and** agreeable;
>
> You are **either** ignorant **or**
> deceitful;
>
> I must **neither** lose my temper **nor**
> shout at strangers;
>
> He is **not only** a rogue **but also** a
> wife-beater.

And 'either' cannot be mixed with 'nor', nor can 'neither' be teamed with 'or'. When these conjunctions link singular subjects together, the verb must be singular:

> **Neither** cottage cheese **nor** lettuce **is**
> fattening.

The last conjunction to need attention is 'than'. Its frequent misuse is the cause of misunderstanding. The problem lies in the choice of case when it is followed by a pronoun:

> Fred loves Daphne more than me.

When that is said, it is open to the hearer to decide whether the speaker loves Daphne or wishes to be loved by Fred. The hearer can always ask, tactfully, for clarification. The reader is less

Putting Things Together

fortunate:

> You are more acceptable to the Board than
> me

will be read as an insulting or unfriendly
statement:

> You are more acceptable to the Board than
> you are to me.

If the pronoun is changed, the whole meaning is
changed:

> You are more acceptable to the Board than
> I.

The first person singular pronoun 'I' stands for
'than I am', and reveals the fact that the speaker
thinks himself less likely to find favour with the
Board if both are candidates for appointment. So
'if Fred loves Daphne more than I', you can be
sure that the speaker thinks that Fred is welcome
to her. To avoid the ambiguity that arises from
the common colloquial muddling of the pronouns,
always write the thought out: 'than it is to me';
'than he loves me'; or 'than I do'.

'Like' is not a conjunction and should never be
used in phrases where 'as' would be more suitable.
It is an adjective when used to mean something
similar:

> in like manner;

> like father, like son;

> like subjects.

It is a preposition in phrases which mean 'in the
manner of' something:

Putting Things Together

The diseaes spread like wildfire;

it fits me like a glove;

he treats her like a child.

When we use colloquial speech, it may be slovenly to say

He doesn't work like I do

or

She throws money about like confetti,

but these constructions are so widely used that they pass unnoticed. After all it would be a dull life if we could not sometimes say we felt 'like going to the pub' and it would be a less colourful one if we never heard someone described as 'carrying on like crazy'. But this is an area where the conventions of written English disallow the use of 'like' as a conjunction. Someone else must work 'as hard as I do', money must be thrown about 'as if it were confetti', we must feel 'as if we should like' to go to the pub and describe the distraught creature as 'carrying on as if he' or 'she were crazy'.

Small Matters: Articles, Prefixes and Suffixes

The **definite article,** 'the' and the **indefinite article,** 'a', are clearly named. 'A cat' is a single member, any member, of a large group of mammals; 'the cat' is a specific cat, one who tears up your seedlings, eats the butter or needs to be put out at night. The articles act like adjectives, but they cannot be spread thinly without changing their meaning: if you see a black cat and

Putting Things Together

a white cat, the reader knows you have seen two cats. If you have seen a black and white cat, you have only seen one. When you are referring to two separate things or people, you must repeat the indefinite article; 'a cat and dog are two different animals' is an ambiguous statement and the 'dog' needs an indefinite article of its own. It is even more important to apply the definite article correctly. When we write 'The Chairman and Managing Director' the reader must be able to assume that the same person holds both offices. If this is not so, we must write 'The Chairman and the Managing Director' in order that two chairs will be provided.

When the definite article comes before two adjectives describing the same thing and there is no possibility of confusion we can either treat the noun as singular and repeat the article before each adjective:

the boxed and unboxed products;

The Old and New Testaments,

or we can write of the 'singular and Plural numbers' or 'the singular and the plural number' in this way, but must find some other way when we deal with 'the black and white cats unless they are all 'black and white' cats. The least cumbersome way is to write of 'the black cats and the white ones'.

Prefixes are·small additions to the beginning of a word to give a contrary or different meaning: 'necessary' becomes 'unnecessary'; we can 'ride' or 'override'; something can be 'written', 'rewritten' or 'underwritten'.

A prefix is only a prefix if it is firmly attached to the word: 'rent', in 'rent collector' is not a

Putting Things Together

prefix, but an adjective. **Suffixes** come at the end of a word, usually changing its shape: 'multiply' becomes 'multiplier' or 'multiplicand'; 'master' can change to 'masterful'; 'ease' to 'easier'; the quality of a 'soft' thing is 'softness'.

Prefixes alter their functions. The suffix, as you can see in the examples above, can turn a verb into a noun, a noun into an adjective or adverb and an adjective into a noun.

What is Left Out: Ellipsis

In colloquial speech, ellipsis is so common that we are unaware of it. It is the omission of words than can, without misunderstanding, be supplied by the reader or hearer:

>   I think he will come

ia an abbreviation of

>   I think that he will come.

It is a useful way of avoiding the repetition of words and of eliminating a pronoun where the sense supplies it:

>   The accountant came to the factory
>   and (he) went over the books;
>
>   One man was finished, the other (man
>   was) finishing;
>
>   I think it a good idea

is understood as

>   I think that it is a good idea.

Putting Things Together

Some words cannot be left out with impunity. To write

> This product is as good or better
> than that

is slipshod; the product should be 'as good as or better' than the thing with which it is compared. But it is falling into ignorant error if you try to lump together a collection of auxiliary verbs which need different parts of the verb to complete their sense:

> I deny that this is, could or has
> occurred.

In that sentence, 'is' needs 'occurring', 'could' needs 'occur' and 'is, could or' makes nonsense of 'occurred'.

Another mistake is to try to make one auxiliary do the work of two. In a short sentence like:

> One dog was muzzled and the others
> chained up,

the sense is so plain that it takes no effort to supply the missing word 'were' after 'others'. If, however, there are too many words separating the first part of the compound sentence from the second, the meaning may not be quite so clear:

> The man was summarily removed from
> the post he held and thereafter his
> friends dismissed or forced to
> resign.

The omission of 'were' after 'friends' leaves a thought hanging in the air. The reader is left looking for the people that the friends 'dismissed or forced to resign', rather than understanding

Putting Things Together

that they were also victims of a purge.

Certain nouns and verbs always require the word 'that' when the following clause contains part of the verb 'to be':

> Our view is **that** ...is, was;
> My opinion is **that** ... is, was;
> My decision is **that** ... is, was;
> We assert **that** something is, was;
> I declare **that** is, was;
> He has decided **that** something is, was;
> They took the view **that** ... was.

The following sentences are all wrong:

> Mr Circumspex asserted he was blameless;

> It was decided the move was beneficial;

> When you state our product is not up to standard, I must disagree.

'Asserted', 'decided' and 'stated' should, in each instance, be followed by 'that'.

Ellipsis can make a writer forget about the case of a pronoun following 'than'. Remember when we say 'You are more qualified than I', we are leaving out the word 'am' after 'I'. In an elliptical statement, the use of the objective 'me', 'her' or 'him' can alter the whole meaning of the statement - or it can display your ignorance.

Putting Things Together

Illegal Entries

It is sometimes tempting to puff up a sentence by using a construction that sounds more elaborate. Sometimes one has started writing a sentence and, when the beginning does not fit the thought that follows, one then tries to complete it rather hastily, regardless of convention. An example of this is the intrusive infinitive:

> No better product is possible to be found.

'Possible' means 'that can be done or happen', so its inclusion with the infinitive makes nonsense of the sentence; 'can' should be substituted for the words 'is possible to'. The same stricture applies to 'probable', for which the word 'likely' must be substituted in similar constructions. You may 'claim to be' something yourself, not 'claim' something else 'to be' something:

> We claim this to be the best product on the market

is wrong. You must 'claim that it is' the best product or find another way of making your claim. In the same way, you can pretend to be Hitler, but not pretend the moon to be madeof cream cheese.

Another popular mixup takes place between words of analogous meaning. You may 'forbid' someone 'to do' something but you may not 'forbid' them 'from doing' it. On the other hand,,you may 'prohibit' them 'from doing' something, but not 'prohibit' them 'to do' it. Someone may be 'witnessed doing' something but 'demand that' they tell it. You will find other examples relating to gerunds and infinitives in the section dealing with the infinitive form of the verb.

Putting Things Together

To Quote or Not to Quote

If we use the exact words used by a speaker, we
are quoting directly; we are reproducing **direct
speech.** But we can also reproduce it indirectly by
altering the pronouns and tenses. Here is an
example of direct speech:

'I shall most certainly give Sophronia a piece
of my mind', the old lady answered. 'Not only is
the stitching giving way in the seams, but the
stuff itself shows signs of wear, which is am
affecting instance of the total inutility of
geography'. (from: John Masefield "The Midnight
Folk", 1927, Heinemann, London)

Here it is turned into **indirect speech:**

The old lady answered that she would most
certainly give Sophronia a piece of her mind.
She said that not only was the stitching giving
way in the seams, but that the stuff itself
showed signs of wear and that this was an
affecting instance of the total inutility of
geography.

Notice that 'she' and 'her' have replaced 'I' and
'my'. The tenses have also shifted into the past.
Direct speech is reported as if the writer and the
reader are both present when the words are being
said. But indirect speech is a report of something
that has already happened and therefore requires a
past tense.

5 EASING THE READER'S PATH

Pauses for Breath - Punctuation

For some writers, there is only one punctuation
mark: the full stop or period. The rest, for them,
is sheer ornament. Others are beguiled by the
ornamental theory and spatter commas at random
throughout their sentence. And there are those who
know that commas have some useful function and
treat them as notation marks for a text that is to
be read aloud. The last group have some justi-
fication for their treatment of commas. But the
real purpose of every mark of punctuation is to
fulfil the writer's purpose: the communication of
information, facts and ideas as clearly as
possible.

The Period or Full Stop

The full stop should never be used to end an incomplete statement, that is, a statement without a
finite verb. Disregard the practices of some
journalists, of which this is a sample:

    A quick glance at the menu suggested
    healthy eating at a reasonable price.

    No fried foods, wholemeal rolls, with a
    typical spot of "petit dejeuner"

being poached eggs on toast with coffee.

If we overlook, for the time being, the muddled and confusing construction of the incomplete statement following the stop, we can still see that it is not a main clause. In fact, it is not a clause of any description but a collection of descriptive terms referring to 'menu' in the previous sentence. At least, one assumes that it refers to 'menu' in spite of ambiguous phrasing. What made the mistake more obvious was the placing of the two 'sentences' in separate paragraphs, a custom increasingly adopted by the journalists of "The Times" now that they feed their copy into machines. Disregard also the style of the airport bookshop authors, many of whom hope to gain an impressionistic effect from a series of disjointed phrases set off by full stops. It is open to writers of fiction to play about to heighten artistic effect, but writers of non-fiction, whether letters, reports or essays, are prohibited from doing so.

The Colon

The colon could be described as a stop somewhat lighter than a full stop and somewhat heavier than a semi-colon, which we shall come to next. It has one definite function; it introduces a promised list. This can be a list which follows the stop sequentially:

There are several reasons why I believe myself to be an ideal marriage partner: I am under thirty, seven-foot tall, keen on sky-diving, have four sisters who live with me and own a motor-cycle and a music centre.

Easing the Reader's Path

Or the stop can preface a more formal list:

    Four bedspreads
    One sheet
    Seven pillowcases
    Two-and-a-half pairs of socks

There are very few places where the colon can be followed by a dash, and even in these it is a fussy-looking device. It is better avoided.

The Semi-colon

It is worth mastering the use of this helpful stop. It signals a pause between closely connected thoughts, each of which deserves attention but needs to be linked by the reader with the other. It is also useful in expressing contrasting ideas, as this passage from Macaulay shows:

> Former princes had raised ship-money only in time of war; it was now exacted in time of peace. Former princes, even in the most perilous wars, had raised ship-money only along the coasts; it was now exacted from the inland shires. Former kings had raised ship-money only for the maritime defence of the country; it was now exacted by the admission of the Royalists themselves, not with the object of maintaining a navy, but of furnishing the king with supplies, which might be increased at his discretion to any amount and expended at his discretion for any purpose.

Don't get carried away with enthusiasm for the semi-colon. It is best used when the statements it links are not too long, and when a conjunction would make the whole over-lengthy and unwieldy. It

Easing the Reader's Path

is usual to say that it is never used when the second statement begins with a conjunction. This stricture needs tempering; the conjunctions that co-ordinate, or join on equal terms, can legitimately be preceded by a semi-colon: 'and', 'or', 'but', 'yet'. They should not be used before a conjunction introducing a dependent clause: 'as', 'since', 'because', 'when', 'if', or 'though'. As the dependent clause literally depends on the main clause, it would be wrong to use a stop strong enough to mark a pause in reading.

As a useful alternative to conjunctions, the semi-colon has a place in paragraphs composed of a number of long complex and compound sentences. Too many 'ands' can wear out a reader's attention. It has the effect of introducing a break in the rhythm of reading in such circumstances. It can also be used to smooth out the jerky effect of too many short sentences.

The Comma

Often misused, often abused, the comma is the most necessary punctuation mark. With the proper employment of commas, the writer can make the reader follow the progress of thoughts. The comma separates the subordinate clauses from the main clause in a sentence. Although a passage without commas sounds dead and its meaning is obscure, commas are not meant to reproduce the inflections of the speaking voice. The pauses and word-stresses used in speaking should be apparent in the rhythm of the clauses and sentences. It is the presentation of thoughts, either in sequence or as asides or insertions, that the comma marks.

Easing the Reader's Path

Its function is to make reading easier:

> The drug, used by dentists and in
> hospitals as an initial anaesthetic, was
> described as addictive and potentially
> dangerous by professor John Robinson, a
> consultant anaesthetist from West
> Midlands Health Authority, who has
> contributed to two medical papers on the
> drug.

The commas allow the adjectival phrases 'used by
dentists and in hospitals as an initial an-
aesthetic', qualifying 'drug', and 'a consultant
anaesthetist from West MIdlands Health Authority',
describing the Professor, to be used close to the
nouns they qualify. A relative clause, 'who has
contributed to two medical papers on the drug',
not only follows the qualifying phrase, but rounds
off the message of the sentence. The main clause
and the additions could have been set out as
separate sentences:

> The drug was described as addictive and
> potentially dangerous by Professor John
> Robinson. Professor Robinson is a
> consultant anaesthetist from West
> Midlands Health Authority. He has
> contributed to two medical papers on the
> drug. The drug is used by dentists and in
> hospitals as an initial anaesthetic.

Making Sense: Commas and No Commas

The comma is used to set off nouns in apposition.
A noun in apposition is one that refers to another
noun, usually one immediately preceding it:

> Armero's once resident clown, Luis

Easing the Reader's Path

> Enrique Moreno, has changed his
> makeup and his act;
>
> Sir Edward Eveleigh, a former Lord
> Justice of Appeal ...;
>
> Miss Bun, the baker's daughter.

Adjectives that pile up the effect are separated by commas:

> This unprincipled, dishonest, deceitful
> rogue;
>
> this lavish, luxurious, expensive
> product.

If, however, the adjectives describe separate qualities, they need no commas:

> an ancient much-chimneyed house;
>
> new colourful washable wallpapers;
>
> a dirty battered old van.

Adverbs and adverbial phrases are set off with commas when to do so has a direct effect on meaning:

> Outside, the castle appeared to be grim
> and forbidding; inside, it was luxurious
> and inviting:
>
> It is seen, politically, as very
> damaging, but it has not yet affected her
> popular image.

In that second example, the commas setting off 'politically' could have been left out, but the

writer has used them to reinforce the strength of
the first statement, ...'seen as damaging', and to
heighten the contrast between the two statements.
Commas are not needed in places where the adverb
or adverbial phrase fits naturally into the
sentence:

> From Paris he travelled to Berlin;

> Already the crowd had gathered;

> In 1986 the profits fell;

> The audience muttered but grudgingly
> applauded.

If you turn the first example round, you can see
why no comma is needed after 'from Paris':

> He travelled to Berlin from Paris.

Commas are equally unnecessary after 'already' and
'in 1986' or about 'grudgingly'. If the adverb, as
in the next example, is qualifying the verb next
to it commas add nothing to the meaning unless
particular emphasis is required.

In lists, the comma is omitted after the pen-
ultimate word:

> The lot consists of an ironing board, a
> pair of steps, two stools and a
> plant-stand;

> A volcanic eruption, flash-floods and mud
> avalanches wiped the town of Armero off
> the map.

If, however, to leave it out would create ambiguity, it must be put in:

Easing the Reader's Path

> There are several estate agents in the
> area: ... Tilley and Noad, Hobbs and
> Chambers, Allens, and Howard.

If there were no comma after Allens, the reader
might take Allens and Howard to be a partnership
like Hobbs and Chambers.

A comma is usually required before "but" when it
introduces a clause that is antithetic to, or
contrasts with, the main clause:

> Life is a gamble, but there aren't many
> winners;

> It would have been a most successful
> occasion, but for the mixup with the
> jelly and the mashed potatoes;

> He likes prunes, but not with gravy.

When the but-clause begins the sentence, it must
be set off by a comma:

> But for the auditor's careful research,
> the fraud would not have been discovered.

Commas are superfluous when "but" is followed by a
simple adjective or an adjective modified by an
adverb:

> She was tired but happy;

> He looked thin but very well.

Commas and Clauses

Clauses beginning with a participle must be set
off by commas. If they are not, it will be

Easing the Reader's Path

difficult for the reader to decide where they
should be applied:

> He watched the child running aimlessly
> and joyfully about the field with
> pleasure.

With commas the sentence has a different meaning:

> He watched the child, running aimlessly
> and joyfully about the field, with
> pleasure.

A comma is still used when the participial phrase
follows the main clause:

> It pleased him to see the child, running
> about the field aimlessly and joyfully.

In the next example the phrase begins the sentence
but is still followed by a comma:

> Running about the field aimlessly, the
> child, and its joy, pleased him.

Notice that the inset phrase 'and its joy' has a
comma before 'and' in order not to diminish the
sense of the main clause, 'the child pleased him'.

If the participial phrase is connected to the
sentence by 'and', take care that the commas are
put in the right place. They should act as
parentheses but are often inserted before the
conjunction, making nonsense of the main clause:

> He tripped, and falling heavily, hit his
> head on the table.

If we remove the parenthetic phrase, 'and falling
heavily', we are left with 'He tripped hit his
head on the table', which is foolish stuff.

Easing the Reader's Path

Obviously 'and' belongs to the main clause, so, 'He tripped and hit his head on the table'. It is only 'falling heavily' that must be set off by commas.

Sense can depend on the placing of a comma. If the reader must have two goes at a sentence to find out what the writer meant, the sentence is badly written. Punctuation is a vital part of making sense. In the following sentence the survivors, or most of them, seem to have been as overwhelmed by the dollars as they were by the natural disasters that befell them:

> Despite the millions of dollars in
> national and international aid that
> poured in the majority of survivors
> remain homeless, unemployed and desperate
> because of bureaucratic chaos.

It was not a very good sentence to start with, but the omission of a comma after 'poured in' makes it even more of a muddle.

In adjective clauses the presence or absence of commas can radically alter meaning. Adjective clauses fall into two groups: defining and non-defining. The defining clause restricts its descriptive action by defining the subject. The non-defining clause does not particularize the subject, merely adding a fact to the sentence. This sounds very complicated but the following examples should make the distinction clear:

> Men with army service who are
> short-tempered should not join the police
> force.

The clause 'who are short-tempered' defines the particular category of ex-Army men unsuited for police work. If the clause were to be set off by

Easing the Reader's Path

commas, the sense would be changed:

> Men with Army service, who are
> short-tempered, should not join the
> police force.

Now something nasty has been said about all the noble chaps who felt drawn to police work. The difference is just as clear in this example:

> A man who was here this morning gave us
> information.

The clause defines the subject, a nameless man who can nevertheless be identified becaue he was in a particular place at a particlar time and only that man. But if we put in commas and make it a non-defining clause, the man, who just happened to be on the premises this morning, is unidentified:

> A man, who was here this morning, gave us
> information.

Try to remember that the non-defining clause would have much the same effect if it were enclosed in parentheses.

So much has now been said about commas that you may feel obliged to pepper work with them, a great mistake. The comma must be used sparingly and only where it contributes to the sense of what you write and to the reader's understanding. There are many places where commas are quite unnecessary. Never, for instance, use them meaninglessly in addresses (5, Pigg Lane, for example). It serves no purpose to do so. Nor is it useful to write 10th December, 1987, unless you are distinguishing the 1987 date from any other December 10th that happens to be floating about. Tell people that you live at 2 The Roundabout and were born on 1st January 1965.

Easing the Reader's Path

The comma, properly used, is the writer's friend. Improperly used it vexes and confuses the reader and produces a messy text. Never try to get yourself out of a badly constructed sentence by putting in a comma to show where the subject ends. Think out the sentence before you write and determine where, if anywhere, commas may be needed.

Inverted Commas

The inverted comas are quotation marks and should always be so described. It is important to remember that they may only enclose the actual words used by someone else. The words within them may not be altered. In particular, the pronouns and tenses must be rendered as they were spoken or written. Take this example:

> One source said: 'If he decides against us, then we will have to consider what step to make next.'

Quite a number of writers feel that it is in order to make a few alterations. They may decide to change 'make' to 'take', forgetting that it is the speaker's right to have his grammar and syntax reproduced exactly. If he chooses to make his steps rather than take them, he may do so with impunity inside the quotation marks. More seriously, some writers fudge the distinction between direct speech (page 94) and indirect speech. They feel that their involvement as a hearer should allow them to edit what they heard:

> One source said: 'If he decided against them, then they would have to consider what step to take next.'

Easing the Reader's Path

If a quotation is to be changed to indirect speech quotation marks must not be used. In the example above, 'they' should have been omitted and the word 'if' should begin with a lower-case letter. The way to avoid making such mistakes is to quote directly only that part of the sentence best said in the speaker's own words:

> One source said that if he decided
> against them, they would have "to
> consider what step to make next."

Newspapers make their own rules. So do the publishers of fiction. Although your typewriter has an enticing key with double quotation marks on it, this is not an encouragement to use them in preference to single inverted commas. The proper custom is to use single quotation marks for all quotations except for quotations within quotations:

> Here the old lady shed a few tears, tried
> to fill her glass from the bottle and,
> finding it empty, sucked its neck
> instead. After a few puffs at her
> cigarette she went on:
>
> 'And he was only at home for two days ...
> this time he went off muttering about the
> tomb. And this time he never came back to
> his poor little Tiney Piney, never,
> never, never, never, never,: Shakespeare.
> Do you ask me: "Was it liver?". No, I
> say, it wasn't liver. He went off in the
> fly, muttering about the tomb and what
> became of him nobody knows.'

It gives an impression of facetiousness to put single words into quotation marks:

> We have been told that this is the

Easing the Reader's Path

'correct' method.

It is only possible to distinguish a word like that if you are making an ironic comment on something. Certainly it is a mistake to use the device to create a playful or lighthearted image. The reader may not respond as you would wish.

Question Marks

Keep question marks for questions. They are used properly in this example:

Have you sent us an invoice?,

but not in this one:

I am writing to ask if you have sent an invoice?

The first is a question; the second is a statement, 'I am writing'. Another sort of mistake is to confuse an imperative statement with a question:

Name me those who love me well
And those who'd see me fry in hell.

That is a concealed command to someone to name something. The fact that the speaker expects to be told that though nobody may love him, he does not have enemies, is irrelevant. However some questions are treated as statements when they should be followed by a question mark:

Will you please answer my letter?

No matter how politely you may put it, you are asking if your correspondent proposes to reply. A certain sort of abstract question is also often

Easing the Reader's Path

deprived of its question mark:

> Would it be believed that consumers,
> faced with new models inferior in quality
> and workmanship to the old, could retain
> a sense of loyalty to a brand-name.

In spite of its length, that is a question, not a statement and should have a question mark instead of a full stop. If you are reporting speech, or writing in a literary style, distinguish between the ex- clamatory statement and the question. In this sentence:

> How often have we seen a star fall!,

the writer seems to indicate that it happens frequently in the entertainment or business world and it is therefore an exclamation. But the same words could be used in a serious question for another night-sky watcher:

> How often have we seen a star fall?

Don't put a question mark inside parentheses (?). In letters, it gives the appearance of school-girlish coyness and the effect is twee. In more formal letters or essays, you either know or don't know whatever it is that you are querying. If it is an attempt to sneer or point the finger, it is snide and a vulgarism. If you really don't know, there are more dignified ways of saying so. The question mark has the strength of a full stop and can end a sentence in its own right. It is never a substitute for an exclamation mark.

The Exclamation Mark

Exclamation marks should be used as little as possible. They are reserved for exclamations. The trouble is that the excited writer often feels a need to show the excitement by decorating a text unnecessarily. This gives the work an uneducated or juvenile look. Exclamations are words used as interjections: Oh! Help! Damn! Gordon Bennet! They include sentences or short statements indicating shock, surprise, sorrow or 'schadenfreude':

> What a comedown! She's gorgeous! How it hurts! How we laughed!

Emotional statement or phrases can be exclamations:

> What fair-weather friends! How could they do it!

Certain wishes:

> God help us! Long live the Queen! Go to the devil!

and insults:

> Poltroon! Boy-racer! Thief! Liar! Swine!

are followed by exclamation marks. I have often wondered why it is more insulting to call someone by a word that is usually a collective noun, 'swine', than to call them Pig! For some obscure reason, the singular pig has become a term of endearment, but it still merits an exclamation mark. The mark, as you see, has a limited use.

Like the question mark, it is never to be put between parentheses. Surprised, astonished or shocked as you may be, and you may wish your reader to be just as shocked as you are, but it is still a vulgar and uneducated thing to do and exasperates the reader.

Easing the Reader's Path

Parentheses and Brackets

Learn to tell these marks apart. Although the familiar round marks ( ) are often called brackets, they are more properly called parentheses. I have spelt the word correctly; because there is a pair of marks, the plural is used. A parenthesis is the matter inserted between the marks. There must always be a pair of marks, the second one completing, or closing, the parenthesis. Brackets, also always found in pairs, are usually comments, corrections or notes added to another writer's work. They are squarer in shape than parentheses. Unless you are annotating someone else's text, you will seldom need them.

The golden rule for parenthetic insertions is to keep them short. If they are too long, you may lose your way and include part of the sentence or, even worse, forget how the sentence began. Long parentheses are difficult for the reader to sort out. If you find that there is a great deal that you must say in the parenthesis, it is better to start the sentence again and use the parenthetic matter either as clauses joined to the main statement by a conjunction or as separate sentences.

Because the parenthesis is an insertion, it does not affect the punctuation of the sentence. If it were not there, and a comma would be required, you must still place the comma after the closing of the parenthesis:

> I do not trust the man (an out-and-out
> rogue), but must use him.

The second half of parentheses is not a stop; it merely closes off the interpolation so a full stop

Easing the Reader's Path

is still needed when the parenthetic matter comes at the end of a sentence:

> I do not trust the man, who is an out-and-out rogue (but I use him).

While one should try to keep parenthetic insertions out of formal letters and other serious work, parentheses are useful in allowing one to put in small bits of information without greatly lengthening the sentence:

> His first marriage (1927) was to a barmaid in Des Moins, Iowa; his second (1928, Washington, D.C.) was to the managing director of an embalming firm. When he tried to marry for the third time (1928, Boston, Mass.), his parents arrived and told the bride (a meat-pie maker's widow of 50) that the boy was not yet 17 years old.

Notice that any matter inside the parentheses is punctuated normally.

Dash It or Don't Dash It

Dashes, like parentheses, come in pairs. They can, in certain situations, be used singly. They can never become triplets; if a sentence has more than two dashes, it is either an outburst of hysteria or an entry in someone's diary. Dashes serve the same purpose as parentheses in marking an insertion:

> When we first began a business relationship with Pobjoys - during my father's time as manager - it was a small firm.

Easing the Reader's Path

They are not there to mark disconnected thoughts which the writer has not troubled to compose assentences. Parentheses snuggle round an insertion like cats' tails; dashes make larger openings in sentences and the insertion has a more disruptive or dramatic effect. Consequently, care is needed in deciding to insert matter between dashes.

Never use the dash as a substitute for a stop. A non-defining relative clause needs commas, not dashes. If a semi-colon is what you need, use it. If you are in any doubt about the punctuation of your sentence, stop and rewrite it. Don't be tempted to use the dash to tack on something you forgot to include.

Where a short phrase is used and you wish to emphasize it, a single dash can set it off from the rest of the sentence, but it must then be ended with a full stop. Remember that the dash is really one of a pair, but, unlike parentheses, a full stop can take the place of the second dash. In using a single dash, therefore, make sure that only the inserted matter, and no other part of the sentence, comes between the dash and the stop. Having said this, I repeat that it can be used to set off short phrases with emphasis:

Customers are looking for products of
high quality - at low prices.
Manufacturers seek to supply their wants
- at high prices.

Hyphens

There are still some copy-editors about who believe that they are performing a service by re-moving all the hyphens from a manuscript. If nobody spots this piece of vandalism in time, the reader will be left to puzzle through sets of nouns used adjectivally, trying to decide what the writer intended. Is 'tax planning lawyer' a command, or does it refer to his special subject, 'tax-planning'? When a advertiser proclaims that his is 'an old established but expanding firm' is he making a break with the past? And the reader must do some sorting out when faced with

> automatic weather stations, manned land stations, four thunderstorms tracking centres and ocean weather ships.

The Met Office has come a long way from the man with the bad corns and the piece of seaweed when it can produce 'automatic weather', put people on land that is deserted, separate ocean weather from any other kind and, last but best, use thunderstorms for tracking 'centres' and the ships doing something about ocean weather.

Hyphens exist so that readers need not take two bites at the cherry to appreciate its flavour. When reading at a normal pace, one should be able to take in a word at a single glance. One needs, also, to be able to see at once the sense in which words are used; a 'much-used proverb' describes the proverb; a proverb that is 'much used' has an adverb, 'much', modifying the verb, 'used'. Hyphens connect words for precision of meaning, marking the difference between a little used notebook and a little-used notebook. The first is a battered affair and the second is almost blank. Certain pairs of words are usually used without hyphens: 'court martial', 'Solicitor General', but when they are used in the possessive case they are joined by hyphens: Court-Martial's decision, the Solicitor-General's office.

Easing the Reader's Path

Hyphens distinguish between words of the same sounds or spelling but different meaning:

They are relaying the floor	Relaying information
A book is re-bound	On the rebound
A re-creation of events	A recreation area
Torn umbrellas re-covered	Lost umbrellas recovered

Hyphens are used to connect the prefixes, anti-, non-, pre-, to words beginning with a vowel and to words that would otherwise confuse the eye. That is the English custom. Webster tried to impose on American usage the omission of hyphens in all cases. I suspect, however, that American writers sensitive to a reader's needs may often insert them to avoid breaks in concentration. On the left are words with hyphens; on the right are the same words according to American usage:

anti-aircraft	antiaircraft
anti-papal	antipapal
anti-alcoholism	antialcoholism
non-jury	nonjury
non-usage	nonusage
non-union	nonunion
pre-acquaint	preacquaint

Easing the Reader's Path

pre-engage	preengage
pre-elect	preelect
pre-eminent	preeminent
pre-operative	preoperative

Some words that have been in use for a long time have lost their hyphens without too much confusion (except among bad spellers).

nondescript	preamble
nonentity	antisocial
nonconformist	antithesis
nonsense	antibody

Hyphens unite compound words where the vowels at the end of the first word and the beginning of the second would distract the reader:

amino-acids	sea-urchin
radio-isotope	de-icing

They connect words which together express a meaning more specific than, or different from, that conveyed by the words separately:

mother-in-law	great-grand-mother
air-to-air	mother-of-pearl
aide-de-camp	anti-mink-farming (adjective)

It is often necessary to have a long descriptive term in which adjectives or adverbs are mixed with words that are also nouns or verbs in their own right. The hyphens in such terms are essential if the reader is not to spend time finding out which words are qualifying and which are being qualified:

> A self-igniting gas cooker
>
> a four-wheel-drive automatic saloon car

Here is an unhyphenated example:

> The Company sponsored sports activities grouped together and placed under one manager enjoyed much success.

If we look at the three examples we can see that it is important to put the hyphens in the right place and to join only the terms that are related. A cooker supplied with self-igniting-gas would keep the Fire Brigade on its toes. If a car had four-wheel drive-automatic or automatic-saloon in the advertising description, you might not think it was a production-line model. Place a hyphen between 'Company' and 'sponsored' and the third example makes sense. It isn't necessary to put a hyphen between 'sports' and 'activities'. The hyphen is there to improve understanding, not to decorate the page. Sense must be the watchword. What happened to a fast disappearing car? Perhaps it made bank robbers invisible too. So it is better to call Petra a 'rose-red city' and to keep hyphens in terms like freezing-point, cast-iron, title-page and trade-union official. Furthermore, to place them so that no meaning is lost requires care and thought:

> He offered to put in a trial-model air-to-water heat-pump system.

Watch out for measurements, ages and time-spans.

Easing the Reader's Path

When such terms are used descriptively, they take hyphens. When they form the predicate, they do not.

a twenty-year-old man	the man is twenty years old
a fourteen-foot-long girder	the girder is fourteen feet long
a six-months engagement	an engagement for six months
a half-inch gap	the gap is half an inch

Remember that half an hour, half a dozen and half an inch never take hyphens. They are also never needed in the names of roads and streets to connect the name of the road with the word 'street' or 'road'. I don't know who invented this meaningless and fly-by-night habit and had hoped that it had gone the way of other bad habits. As it still crops up, it is worth pointing out that one ought never to write Silver-street for Silver Street or Ponsonby-road for Ponsonby Road.

Certain types of road-directions do need hyphens. They are often awarded their hyphens in the wrong place, with bewildering results. If you tell someone that the Malmesbury Cricklade-Swindon Cirencester roads meet at Cricklade, you are really misleading them. The hyphen belongs to the road that joins two places together, not between the two roads:

> The Malmesbury-Cricklade
> Swindon-Cirencester roads meet at
> Cricklade.

It is even more important to put them in the right

place when you are connecting two two-word place names:

the Chipping-Norton Stony-Stratford road.

Having said that, I dislike the practice of saving space or words by using the names of the places it connects as the name of the road. It is always preferable to give people clear directions:

The Malmesbury-to-Cricklade and
Swindon-to-Cirencester roads meet at
Cricklade.

If the phrase 'the road from Chipping Norton to Stony Stratford' is used, one avoids the in-congruity of putting hyphens into two unhyphenated place names.

A final word about. hyphens must be devoted to the vexed question of plurals. Some hyphenated titles are indissoluble, for example

Major-General, Lieutenant-General and
Drum-Major.

The plurals are

Major-Generals, Lieutenant-Generals and
Drum-Majors,

because they represent different kinds of Generals and Majors. But as the Adjutant-general is a chap who does the dashing about for the General, a gathering of such men consists of Adjutants-general. It is the chief word in these hyphenated combinations that changes in the plural:

aides-de-camp, Courts-Martial, mothers-in-law, great-grandmothers, fleurs-de-lis, poets-laureate and men-of-war.

Apostrophes

The apostrophe, like the dash, often finds itself stuffed in to take the place of thought. The writer faced with an awkward possessive may feel that he can indicate it in all cases by adding an apostrophe and 's'. Would that it were so. But we must face the fact that the apostrophe stands for something that has been left out. Putting one in unnecessarily shows that the only thing left out seems to be between your ears.

In discussing possessive pronouns, I have already pointed out that the possessive 'its' has no apostrophe. This is also true of 'his', 'hers', 'ours' and 'theirs'; nothing has been left out so there is no need for an apostrophe. When we put an apostrophe and 's' after a noun, it signifies that we have followed modern custom and left out a letter. In Old English nouns had a possessive case; for most nouns this was shown by adding '-es' to the word. The apostrophe shows that the 'e' has been omitted. This is now applied to all nouns, whether they have come to us from Old English or not. There was also an idiomatic use of 'his' after the noun to show possession: 'the child his book', a somewhat literary idiom. Both these forms decayed with time, leaving the apostrophe with 's' to do their work.

The apostrophe, then, can be used to show the possessive case of a noun: Fred's bike, Mollie's mangle. And it is used to show that we have left something out in 'it's'. Since this is the corruption of 'it is', an apostrophe is in order. It is necessary, if one is to avoid making an ignorant mistake, to remember that the possessive of "it" never has an apostrophe.

Easing the Reader's Path

Some writers appear to have a nervous feeling about things which look plain. JUst a little something added will dress up the page a bit. So perfectly acceptable and correct forms like 1980s, the 60s, the low 30s Fahrenheit are given some decorations in the form of apostrophes. It is a silly habit and quite meaningless. If we talk about 'the fashion of the 1930s' we are already using a possessive construction 'of the', and the phrase becomes nonsense if it is written as 'the fashion of the 1930's'. Don't put in apostrophes for the sake of prettiness. You might just as well put green polka dots all over the page.

6 GETTING IT ON PAPER

Stop, Look and Listen

Before you start to write anything, decide what
you need to say. Identify the most important fact
that you intend to pass to someone else. If you
are selling someone a coat, the fact that it is an
outer garment to keep the body warm or dry is more
important than anything else. You may have to
decide whether the reader will know that a coat
can be expected to have a sleeve for each arm. If
it is a garment for a horse or a dog rather than a
human being, you should make this clear at the
outset. Later steps deal with the character of the
coat: the cloth and lining, whether it wraps or
fastens, the size, the length and the price.

Even the simplest message needs some thought. To
leave a note saying that you are leaving home because you can't bear it any longer is footling. If
what you wish is to live by yourself, say so. It
may save you from pursuit. If, on the other hand,
you might choose to stay or return if the other
inhabitants mended their ways, tell them what is
driving you from the hearth, be it the way your
jeans are washed, Uncle's habit of snapping his
false teeth or the inhuman custom of serving fish
pie when everybody knows that you hate it.

When the message contains an instruction on which

Getting it on Paper

the reader is supposed to act, the need for
definition is even greater. From the garbled instruction book to the ill-written order for a subordinate, confused instructions can wreak havoc,
cause physical injury or lose a battle.

Regard the receiver of the message. If the situation were reversed, what would you, as reader,
want or need to know? And what would increase or
decrease your understanding of the information?
When you say something, will the reader attach the
meaning to it that you do? Effective composition
begins with your own clear understanding of what
must be said and the effect you wish it to have on
the reader.

All the Little Bones

There may be people who hold that archaeologists
and palaeontologists have boring occupations - all
fiddle-de-dee and little bones. Archaeologists and
palaeontologists wouldn't agree. The careful work
of finding and putting together all the right
scraps to reconstruct a Greek drinking vessel or a
brontothere is pleasing to do and satisfying when
well done. It is a skilled task and success depends on recognizing the significance of each
small part in its relation to the whole.

The small parts of composition are words. The
words you use are your starting point. You need
only as many as will serve your purpose of conveying information usefully. Bits which do not fit
into the shape of the vase or drinking vessel are
discarded by the expert restorer. Too many bits
will make the job harder; only those that can be
matched together properly can achieve the result.
Sticking in every piece you find will produce
something grotesque. The writer must put aside the
temptation to use the whole of his or her

vocabulary and overdress the message. Wallowing in too many words confuses composition. The quantity of words needs regulation as much as their quality.

Life would be much simpler if it were possible to do away with written composition and just think messages at other people. There would, of course, be no privacy in a wholly telepathic world. Hundreds of tiny irrelevant, irreverent, unimportant, even embarrassing, thoughts are buzzing around in each person's brain. Total communication would be unbearable; a merciful God put a stop to it when the tower was under construction at Babel.

Utterance, spoken or written, controls unlimited thought, or should do so. Some of us, when asked to put something in writing, cannot help flooding the issue with words. If this is not put right, the wretched reader will bob about helplessly on the incomprehensible torrent. Try to state things, when you begin, in the simplest terms you can find. Leave expansion or embroidery until you have finished and can see where improvements are really necessary. If you cannot write simply at the start, you must learn to edit your work. Read it through for sense and clarity and ruthlessly discard superfluous words.

Your choice of words needs discrimination. Good writing gets straight to the point. Simplicity and lucidity go hand in hand. Short familiar simple words used economically are usually best. It has to be said, however, that there is a good deal of nonsense written about choosing Anglo-Saxon words in preference to words derived from the Roman, about choosing short rather than long words and about avoiding polysyllables. The basic advice is right and will, if you keep it in mind, be helpful. Nevertheless, it can be taken to extremes. The word you choose must be the right one

Getting it on Paper

whether or not it comes from Latin, has more than two syllables and is an abstract term.

When you write a word, you must be sure that the meaning it holds for you will be the meaning it holds for your reader. This might seem to be self-evident as far as English-users divided by the Atlantic are concerned. The meanings of a number of words have diverged since the language was first exported. Wherever English is used, local meanings gradually attach themselves to words and this is true of Australia, India and probably Sri Lanka, Nigeria and Singapore. In writing letters to English-speakers abroad, the wisest course is to use words strictly according to the definition given in a standard dictionary.

Even within home territory, people do not always mean the same thing when they use the same word. This can be put down to an inelegant attempt to be smart; the trendy person who insists on using the American spelling 'program' at all times can lead the reader down the wrong path. In Britain 'program' is reserved exclusively for software – computer program – and in every other instance the word is spelt 'programme'. Another area of confusion is the weighting of certain words. To one writer the word 'anticipate' may mean 'to look forward to something'; to another, it means 'to forestall', and its use may indicate that someone is trying to steal a march on someone else. Words that are often used loosely, rather than in their absolute sense, are 'responsible', 'purport', 'valid' and 'erode'. One could fill a page with examples, usually words that are intended to make the writer's statement be taken seriously. Casual over-use of heavyweight words only debases them. If you are forever 'protesting in the strongest terms' people will stop paying any attention. Some writers seize on a word that they hear and proceed to use it in the wrong context. 'Feasible' does

Getting it on Paper

not mean 'possible' with any sense of uncertainty and it should not be used for the state of something that might or might not come to pass. 'Feasible' means 'practicable", 'capable of being done'. A 'protagonist' is not the opponent of an 'antagonist'. The protagonist is the actor taking the chief part so it is plainly useless to say 'the chief protagonist'. It can be used in the plural if, for example, you wish to refer to the most visible or important persons attending a meeting. Pay attention to the social overtones of words. 'Questionable' is an apparently straight-forward word; it means 'open to question' or 'capable of being questioned'. Unfortunately, to many people it means 'suspicious' rather than 'arguable', 'dubious' rather than 'doubtful'.

Connecting the Dry Bones

The sentence forms a single thought unit:

> God is good:
> Bad oysters make people sick.

A sentence does not have to be a bald statement. The core of the sentence, the main statement, can be expanded by adding phrases and subordinate clauses. If two statements are very closely connected and form part of one thought or idea they can be joined by a conjunction. Nevertheless the thought conveyed by the sentence should be effectively a single idea.

There is no 'ideal' length for a sentence. On the whole, short sentences are the most direct way of conveying information. The brief statement is easier to read and interpret. Short statements carry an argument along, punching it home. Simple statements inform withput ambiguity and make instructions clear. The more a statement is

magnified, the greater the chance of
misunderstanding.

The short sentence, however, tends to lack
subtlety and colour. Life is not all a matter of
informing or instructing. There are times when we
need to persuade or assuage someone. It may be
necessary to soften an otherwise harsh remark or
to relax the mood. Sometimes the reader must be
tempted to read on. Something more must be added
to the plain statement. While you should always
regard conciseness as a virtue, you must not let
it rule your entirely.

The order of words in a sentence is not laid down
by rule. We can choose between the usual word
order:

> Romance at short notice was her
> specialty,

or an inversion:

> Of the former school was Lulu,
> Duchess of Dulverton.

We can join short clauses together:

> She acquired the invention and bought
> the apparatus,

or longer clauses:

> As a mere child he had been precocious-
> ly brilliant; he had declined the editor-
> ship of the <u>Anglian Review</u> at an age when
> most boys are content to have declined
> <u>mensa</u>, a table, and though he could not
> claim to have originated the Futurist
> movement in literature, his <u>Letters to a</u>
> <u>possible Grandson</u>, written at the age of

fourteen had attracted considerable
notice.

You may say one thing while apparently saying
another:

At college his career was of course
highly creditable. An here he prepared
himself for public life ... by studying
the ancient and modern orators with great
assiduity, and by speaking unceasingly at
the debatinġ societies. But though he had
a fine flux of words, and delivered his
little voice with great pomposity and
pleasure to himself, and never advanced
any sentiment or opinion which was not
perfectly trite and stale, and supported
by a Latin quotation; yet he failed somehow, in spite of a mediocrity which ought
to insured any man a success.
(W. M. Thackeray, 1848, Vanity Fair)

You can include a number of things in the subject
of your sentence:

His secluded wife ever smiling and
cheerful, his little comfortable
lodgings, snug meals and homely evenings
had all the charms of novelty and
secrecy.
(W. M. Thackeray, 1848, Vanity Fair)

It is sometimes useful to do a good packaging job,
and fit several relevant facts into one sentence:

Edward Dale, the junior of the house, who
purchased the spoons for the firm, was,
in fact, very sweet on Amelia and offered
for her in spite of all.
(W. H. Thackeray, 1848, Vanity Fair)

Getting it on Paper

And you may save the best for last:

> "No one who has lived in Yom," said
> Crosby fervently, "and remembers its
> green hills covered with apricot and
> almond trees, and the cold water that
> rushes dpwn like a caress from the upland
> snows and dashes under the little wooden
> bridges, no one who remembers these
> things and treasures the memory of them
> would ever give up a single one of its
> unwritten laws and customs."
> (Saki, 1914, Beasts and Super-Beasts)

You may also contrast two ideas by placing them
in antithesis, balancing them in the same
sentence:

> Their thoughts are often new, but seldom
> natural; they are not obvious, but
> neither are they just; and the reader,
> far from wondering that he missed then,
> wonders more frequently by what
> perverseness of industry they were ever
> found.
> (Samuel Johnson, 1781, Life of Cowley)

A certain self-control is needed. It is easy to
fall into bad habits and perpetually produce
sentences of the same sort. And if these sentences
are of the more complicated sort, the effect will
be tediously literary at best, and pompous at
worst. Antithesis, for instance, is like throwing
a stick for a dog. You throw the stick for the
reader and back he or she comes, stick in mouth.
But readers, unlike dogs, quickly tire of the
game. Stick-and-carrot sentences, where the reader
must brave the stick before grasping the carrot at
the end, can be particularly tiresome in quantity.
Once the reader has learned that the important bit

129

Getting it on Paper

is always at the end of the sentence, he can learn to skip over the words that come before it.

It can help in composing sentences if you imagine yourself to be speaking and write down what you say. You can smooth out any roughness later. What matters is that you are writing naturally. And this is the goal you should strive for. Let the sentences flow as if there were a listener, correct any mistakes, make sure that the meaning is clear and you will find that what you write is a reflection of your personality.

Giving Life to the Dry Bones

If the sentence is the expression of a single idea, the paragraph is a collection of ideas about a single theme. The sentences should have the same relationship to the paragraph as the sleeves, back, fronts and pockets have to a whole jacket: parts of one thing. Paragraphs form the essential steps in the presentation of a report. They make stages in the logical argument or the essay. In letters, it is customary to put the introductory or greeting sentences and the closing sentiments, whether minatory or friendly, into separate paragraphs. The paragraphs in the middle of the letter can then deal with the writer's intentions in an unfettered way.

This does not mean that you should set out to compose paragraphs in a solemn, deliberate and formal way, as if you were composing a sonnet or a sonata. If you do, the result will be stagey and self-conscious, all that is meant when one refers to a 'literary' style in a disparaging way. Like sentences, paragraphs should flow naturally from your own ordered thought-processes. And, like sentences, they can be smartened up or re-arranged at a later stage. Naturalness is the essence of

Getting it on Paper

prose composition.

Perhaps you did not think that you were writing prose. If so, the bad news is that if you write as trivial a thing as a note to yourself:

> Don't forget to call Mother tonight
> after 8:00,

you are writing prose. If you write anything other than poetry, it comes out as prose. Even what you say, unless you always burble in rhymed couplets, is prose. It is time the poor thing lost its bad name, acquired through decades of resistance to a subject called Prose Composition.

The Victorian era often seems to have been characterized by a zealous pursuit of order. Almost anything could be brought under control by a set of rules or precepts. Essay-writing and letter-writing suffered from the belief that there was a single right way in which they could be done. Instead of getting rid of the constrictions, educationists in the post-war era chopped down the bridge and threw it into the river because they felt it was too narrow.

If you wish to use writing as a tool of communication, you musy follow the middle way. Understand what you are doing. Think about the order in which information needs to be given. Express yourself in clear statements. Start a new paragraph when you move on to a fresh idea or another stage in your argument. Read what you have written and correct or improve it as a final step before signing it or handing it in.

It used to be said that it must be possible to express the theme of a well-constructed paragraph in a single sentence. Unless you are proposing to precis your own work, you should not let this idea worry you. Regard it as a reminder of the need for unity in a paragraph. And you will find that in planning the sequence of your narrative or argument, there is one statement which is the key to the theme or topic of a paragraph.

When the key statement is made at the beginning of the paragraph, the statements that follow expand or elaborate it. The paragraph must be closed when the amplificaton is complete. Sometimes the sentences in a paragraph are like a pathway leading to the statement at the end. Occasionally these methods are combined when a statement needs first to be introduced, then amplified. Whatever th form of the paragraph when you come to write it, remember that the guiding principle is coherence. A collection of stray and disconnected statements is not a paragraph; it is a mess.

Obviously paragraphs consist of more than one sentence. At this point, the way in which information is conveyed needs attention. Just as we select words from our vocabulary to express ourselves, so we choose the sentence types which will keep the reader's interesr or attention fixed.

Brevity is a good thing, but too many short sentences produce a choppy effect. Avoid making the reader sea-sick by varying the length. Here acaulay has put short sentences between complex statement. It has the effect of focusing the attention on important pieces of information:

> It not seldom happens that serious
> distress and danger call forth, in beauty
> and deformity, heroic virtues and abject
> vices which, in the ordinary intercourse
> of good society, might remain during many
> years unknown even to intimate
> associates. Under such circumstances met

Warren Hastings and the Baroness Imhoff,
two persons whose accomplishments would
have attracted notice in any court of
Europe. The gentleman had no domestic
ties. The Lady was tied to a husband for
whom she had no regard, and who had no
regard for his own honour. An attachment
sprang up, which was soon strengthened by
events such as could hardly have occurred
on land. Hastings fell ill. The Baroness
nursed him with womanly tenderness, gave
him his medicines with her own hand, and
even sat up in his cabin while he slept.
Long before the Duke of Grafton reached
Madras, Hastings was in love.

There is no need to emulate Macaulay's Victoria
style. He is, however, a master of the art of
pacing. The occasional long and complex sentence
is necessary and interesting, but readers get
bored when they must ever and again grope their
way to the end of a labyrinth.

If you cannot form the habit of thinking out
sentences before setting them down, then you must
re-read your work carefully. Vary the length of
your sentences as part of the final editing
process.

Dry Bones Dancing

All that has ben said ·so far about the
construction of sentences and paragraphs applies
to any written work as a whole. The substance of
what you have written must, when it reaches the
reader, say what you intend as clearly as if you
were there in person. The words should be right,
the paragraphs coherent and the argument or
message lucid. What you have to say should follow

Getting it on Paper

a logical progression from the introducton to the close, with ideas in the right sequence for understanding.

When you have come to the end of what you have written, the work begins. Unless you are writing yourself a note, always re-read things before they leave your hands. Look first at the sequence of ideas and re-arrange them in order if necessary. Examine the structure of paragraphs and make sure that they, like the sentences in them, vary in length to maintain interest. Since you began, better words to express your thoughts may have come to you. Now is the time to improve clarity.

Last of all, cut. Be ruthless. Go through the whole piece and eliminate any superfluous word or bit of cleverness that doesn't really advance your theme. Read your work aloud and see if it sounds natural. Remember that if it can't be read aloud with ease, it certainly won't be attractive to the reader. The editing process applies at all times, even in the examination room. Try to allow time to cross out and improve what you have written in haste. A capacity for self-criticism will do more to please examiners, readers and even publishers than neat but incoherent outpourings.

7 A FAIRLY STRAIGHT AND NARROW PATH

No Getting Away With It

Orthographical inaccuracy, bad spelling, is a widespread problem. On the whole it does often seem a greater problem for the native English-speaker than it is for Americans or for those who learn English as a foreign language. Yet a mis-spelt word can either annoy the reader or raise a laugh where none is intended. Moreover, to spell badly is often taken as an indication of lack of education or positive dimwittedness. Cheer up, if you are a poor speller. Many great writers could not spell for toffee. Take further comfort from the fact that it is not too difficult to improve your ability to spell.

The Quickness of the Ear Deceives the Eye

English spelling, for English speakers, presents two awkward areas. Firstly, vowel sounds vary considerably in dialects and regional speech. If you have to rely solely on your ear, the word, as you write it, may look totally unfamiliar to someone from another part of the country. Secondly, English, like fly paper, has acquired a lot of additional material. Words have come in from languages that represent sounds in a way quite different from the mixture of Anglo-Saxon,

A Fairly Straight and Narrow Path

Norman French and Latin that forms the basis of English. The same set of letters may result in several different pronunciations.

Do not sit back and hope for a magic spelling-reform programme that will save you the trouble of learning to make a better job of spelling. The complexities of revising every dictionary and every book that deals with accepted forms of words, to say nothing of finding a committee that would be able to agree on forms and would also be acceptable to all those academics not on such a committee, have frightened off almost everone who has dreamed of a future with "Newspell".

To overcome difficulties presented by regional variation in sounds, the eye, rather than the ear, must govern the way a word is spelt. To do this effectively, one must associate the meaning of the word with its written appearance. This sounds as if one will be forced to consult the dictionary for every word one intends to write. It only applies, however, to those words with which one has difficulties or about which one feels un-certain. Furthermore, the simpler words or hom-ophones should not need more than one dip into the dictionary. The important thing is to connect the meaning and the look of the word.

Just the same basic method is used to deal with the words which represent similar sounds in different ways. The meaning must dictate the spelling. This does not mean that whole chunks of the dictionary will have to be committed to memory. Rather, it indicates the sort of pause for thought that will remind one that the branch of a tree is a longer word, ending in 'ough', than the respectful bend of the head or torso, ending in 'ow'. See the word; don't hear it.

A Fairly Straight and Narrow Path

Never Push Your Luck

Bad guesses in spelling bring no rewards. Instead, every spelling mistake loses points for the writer whether it occurs in a business letter, an examination paper or copy for a publisher. You have, in fact, a better chance of being forgiven for some minor errors in an examination than you will ever get in the harsh world of industry and commerce.

Occasionally, most people, including this writer, need to refresh their memories of certain endings, as in "appearance", 'independence', 'irresistible' or 'irreparable'. Only lexicographers, the dictionary-makers, are immune from the need to dip into the reference book from time to time. And who knows what lexicographers do when no one is watching? The point is that in all circumstances you should check the spelling of any word about which you feel uncertain.

Some very bad spelling is due to lethargy and lack of thought, but some is due to a genuine learning difficulty. If you can read with ease, watch for words used in their proper context. Unless you have a serious reading problem, there is no real excuse for writing 'witch' or 'wich' when you mean to write 'which', or using 'their' when you mean 'there'. These are crude mistakes. If you tend to make them, discipline yourself to look, when reading, at the shapes of words and relate them to the sense in which they are used. Practise by putting together simple sentences and checking the spelling of each word you have used in the dictionary.

Never use a word unless you are quite certain of its meaning. Uncertainty about meaning means, once again, a trip to the dictionary and there, before the definition, is the correct spelling. A careful use of unfamiliar words should help you to avoid a

A Fairly Straight and Narrow Path

reputation for slapdash spelling.

Pitfall Country

It is easy to come to grief over the silent
letters. The silent 'P' in **psychology** or
psephologist comes as no surprise to anyone who
reads newspapers. A little thought may be needed
for **pneumonia** and **pterodactyle** is definitely
dificult. Nevertheless, many of us know that there
is a hidden menace, probably a silent letter 'p',
lurking about these words.

There is a greater degree of uncertainty about
words beginning with a silent 'g' or 'k'. The man
who wrote that he was ' **knawed** by anxiety' was
plainly under stress. Fortunately there are only a
few words in general use that need care. Try
remembering that

> the gnarled gnome, sitting on a piece of
> gneiss, gnashed his teeth at a gnat which
> was gnawing a gnu.

Knock-knees, knives, knickers and knotted knitting
are trouble-free examples of the silent 'k'.

But don't forget

> the knell tolled by the bell;
> the knacker who buys horses for
> slaughter;
> the knave who picks pockets;
> the kneading of bread;
> the knoll on the horizon;
> the knurl that is a knob.

Not all silent letters come at the beginning of
the word. When the silent letter is buried, the
stumbling block can be the sound of the word. As I

A Fairly Straight and Narrow Path

have already said, sound is a false guide to correct spelling. 'To **climb** a ladder' or 'place a **climbing** plant against a wall' are everyday activities. It is still confusing to hear the sounds **numb** and **dumb** and then give a different silent letter to **column** although it has the same sound. One bad speller who had trouble with such words kept a notebook in which he recorded the correct spelling of any word which had given him problems. The mere act of writing the words tended to fix the right spelling in his mind.

In English we can rely on the hard sound of 'c' when it comes before 'a', as in **cash and carry,** and before 'o', as in **compass**, or 'u', as in **cunning.** When 'c' comes before 'e', as in **cellulose** or 'i', as in **cinder**, it has a soft 's' sound. However, when 'c' is combined with 'h', the sound can vary. **Character** has a hard 'k' sound; 'ch' in **chop** and **change** has the same sound as the 't' in 'future'; but **chaperon** has the soft 'sh' sound found in **shop.**

Words whose sound may not give the clues to their spelling could be sought under more than one letter, or a combination of letters. The strange word beginning with the sounded letter "t" that does not appear under 'T' in the dictionary may be found under 'p' and turn out to be 'ptarmigan'. There is no need to despair. Relatively few words begin with silent letters and they will all be found under 'p', 'g', 'k' or 'w'.

Poor spellers worry about the silent letters that come within⋅ the word. Here once more, the dictionary solves the problem and this time the word can be found under the sounded initial letter. The shapes of words like "lamb" and "debt" are so familiar that there is little need for a conscous effort to remember the silent letters. Quite a lot of people, however, make a mess of the

A Fairly Straight and Narrow Path

word 'receipt' unless they write it frequently in the course of their work. They tend to be so busy remembering the silent 'p' that they forget that the 'e' needs to come before the 'i'

The Careless or Occasional Sinner

To be a really bad speller is a misfortune. If you are merely a careless speller you are, not to mince words, either lazy or stupid or both. It is very little trouble to look up the word and assure yourself that you have got it right.

Many careless mistakes happen when a word is changed by a prefix, added at the beginning of the word, or a suffix, added at the end of the word. The purpose of the prefix or suffix is to turn the word to another use:

there has been an accident;

it was broken by accident;

the breakage was accidental;

it was broken accidentally,

or

I engage the gear;

the troops engaged in battle;

the handle was disengaged;

she was re-engaged as secretary;

it was the final engagement of the war.

These changes are governed by a fairly simple set

of rules, designed to ensure that words have one
or, at the most, two accepted spellings. If all
the writers of English spelt every word according
to their own personal system, most written work
would be largely unintelligible. The rules are
there to keep us out of trouble.

Like most rules, there are exceptions. If you find
the rules hard to remember, try remembering the
exceptions. It is easier to recall a rule through
the things which break it.

The most familiar prefixes are those which give a
negative or opposite meaning to a word and those
which imply that something is repeated or returned
to a former state. There are also the prefixes
which give the sense of something done beforehand
and of something moved down or away from its usual
state:

Prefixes negating the sense:

    in- as in: incorrect
                    ineligible

    il- as in: illegal
                    illegible

    im- as in: immortal
                    immobilize

    ir- as in: irreconcilable
                    irrelevant,

    un- as in: unjustifiable
                    unbelievable

Prefix indicating a return to a former state:

A Fairly Straight and Narrow Path

    re- as in: reassure
                  recharge
                  rekindle
                  repossess

Prefix indicating repetition:

    re- as in: repaper
                  retrial
                  recapitulate
                  reincarnate

Prefix indicating something done beforehand:

    pre- as in: predigest
                  preconceive
                  predecease
                  precondition

Prefix indicating a move down or away from a usual
state:

    de- as in: decentralize
                  decompose
                  depolarize
                  deoderize

    dis- as in: dishonour
                  displace
                  disqualify
                  dissatisfy

We also have 'anti-', 'semi-', 'non-' and other
lesser prefixes.

Failure to remember or see that a prefix is in-

volved can lead to a mistake. If the prefix ends
with the same letter that begins the attached
word, then both must go in:

necessary	unnecessary
relevant	irrelevant
liberal	illiberal
moderate	immoderate

There may also be a punctuation problem. Where the
prefix ends in a vowel and the attached word
begins with one, a hyphen may be needed (see
Hyphens, pp 113 - 119). The reader's eye must not
be confused by a word which looks as if it might
mean something else: 're-educate', not
'reeducate'; 're-enact', not 'reenact'.

Suffixes are more likely to bring sorrow or shame
to the writer. Many English words end in a mute
'e' and the possibility of bringing two vowels
into conflict with each other is great in
consequence. The most common suffixes are those
that change the forms of the verbs and those that
make nouns from verbs, adjectives from verbs and
nouns, and adverbs from adjectives.

Verb changes:	-ed	-e
	-ing	-en
Other suffixes:	-ible	-y
	-able	-ion
	-ment	-lese
	-ly	,-ful

Most words give little trouble; the suffix seems
to clip on easily:

pain	cord
painful	corded
painless	cording

A Fairly Straight and Narrow Path

```
deep        impeach
deeper      impeachable
deeply      impeachment
```

Now for the rules and their exceptions.

A. When a word ends in a single vowel, followed
    by a consonant, the consonant **is doubled** be-
    fore a suffix that begins with a vowel. This
    sounds more complex than it is:

```
dig         digging
put         putting
```

The exceptions to A are:

```
houses      gases
```

A1. If the word has more than one syllable and
     the stress comes on the first syllable, the
     consonant **is not** doubled:

```
happen      happening
market      marketing
lucid       lucidity
```

A2. When A1 applies but the word ends in "l", the
     consonant **is** doubled:

```
level       levelled
enthral     enthralling
```

The exceptions to A2 are:

```
parallel   paralleled
```

and where the suffix is '-ish', '-ist' or '-ism'.

A3. When A and A1 apply, but the word ends in

A Fairly Straight and Narrow Path

'p', the consonant **is** doubled:

whip	whipped
kidnap	kidnapper
slip	slipping

The exceptions to A3 are

gallop	galloping
chirrup	chirruped
gossip	gossipy

A4.   If the stress comes on the last syllable, the consonant **is** doubled:

remit	remittance
rebut	rebuttal
occur	occurrence

B.   If there are two vowels before the final consonant, the consonant **is not** doubled:

pool	pooled
wail	wailing
sail	sailor

There are two exceptions to B:

wool	woollen
dial	dialled

C.   Words of more than one syllable which end in 'y' change the 'y' to 'i' before all suffixes **except those beginning with 'i'**:

daisy	daisies
defy	defiant

but

         apply   applying
         copy   copying

C1. Words of one syllable which end in 'y', **keep
    the 'y'**:

         shy   shyly
         spry   spryness

The exception to C1 is 'dry' which changes
according to meaning:

         dry   dryness
                    drier
                    hairdryer

D. A number of words end with a mute 'e'. The
    general rule is that they **keep the 'e' when
    the suffix begins with a consonant** and **abandon
    it when the suffix begins with a vowel**:

    sense   senseless   sensible
    incite   incitement   inciting

D1. Adjectives which already have a suffix-ending
    of -able or -ible **abandon 'le' before the
    suffix '-ly'**:

         compatible   compatibly
         justifiable   justifiably
         admirable   admirably

D2. When D applies but the mute 'e' is preceded
    by a soft 'c' or 'g' **the 'e' is kept before
    suffixes beginning with 'a' or 'o'**:

         peaceable   outrageous
         traceable   manageable

A Fairly Straight and Narrow Path

>   engageable   replaceable

Notice the different sound of 'implacable' but remember to keep the 'e' in 'blameable'.

D3. When a distinction has to be made between words which would look alike when joined to a suffix, **the 'e' is kept before 'i':**

sing - singing	singe - singeing
die - dying	dye - dyeing
ting - tinging	tinge - tingeing

House Rules and Personal Choice

In some circumstances you may find that you are required to spell words in a particular way although your dictionary shows an alternative that you prefer. Bite on the bullet and do as you are told. The only time when you can argue for your own choice is when you are not being paid or published.

The Oxford University Press and all who follow its conventions (laid down in the Oxford Dictionaries) keep the 'e' in 'judgement', 'acknowledgement' and 'abridgement'. If, on the other hand, you must follow Cambridge, these must be spelt 'judgment', 'acknowledgment' and 'abridgment'.

Both Oxford and Cambridge favour '-ize' endings for nouns-turned-verbs, for complete nouns like 'canal - canalize', for nouns ending in 'y' and for nouns whose stems can take '-ism', '-izes', '-ization':

criticism	- criticize
agony	- agonize
civilization	- civilize

A Fairly Straight and Narrow Path

decimal	– decimalize
baptism	– baptize
sympathy	– sympathize
collectivism	– collectivize
epitome	– epitomize

Luckily there are fewer '-ise' endings, notably those words where '-is' is part of the noun stem. Here is a selection:

advertise	excise
advise	improvise
chastise	prise
compromise	surmise
despise	merchandise
disguise	franchise
incise	televise

However the problems posed by the conventions of different spelling systems do not end there. Academic rules are as inconsistent as any in existence. The Concise Oxford Dictionary includes some words like 'aggrandizement – aggrandize' and 'recognition – recognize' because, according to Hart's Rules for Compositors and Readers (published, of course, by Oxford), they are 'assimilated to verbs in -ize'. If you are faced with following the Oxford convention, then you should acquire The Oxford Dictionary for Writers and Editors. You will find it useful in any case as it lists the correct spelling for just about every awkward word you can think of.

There is a group of words which tempt the unwary into mistakes. Words like 'analyse', 'paralyse' and 'catalyse' must never be given a 'z' in an English spelling. 'Lys' is part of the word and must remain so.

In case you thought the ones mentioned so far were

A Fairly Straight and Narrow Path

the only troublesome ones you might encounter, be prepared for the American conventions. You probably already know about 'center' and 'theater'. American spelling also awards an '-ize' ending to all words that do not have it in the English spelling. And the words 'analyse', 'paralyse' and 'catalyse' are spelt 'analyze', 'paralyze' and 'catalyze'. What is more, rules A1 and A2 do not apply; 'leveller' would be spelt 'leveler' and 'kidnapper' appears as 'kidnaper', while that old stumbling-block 'jewellery' is reduced to 'jewelry'.

Although I have adhered to the Oxford convention in this book many English publishers have despaired of its observance by modern printers. A great many books now appear with no distinction made between '-ize' and '-ise' endings. All verbs are given the '-ise' ending. That this should be the opposite of the American custom only illustrates the difficulties of finding one acceptable, universal, system.

If you can choose to follow your own inclinations, remember that whether you put the 'e' into 'judgment' or write 'recognise' rather than 'recognize', whatever you choose should be found in one dictionary or another. Moreover, if you have your own choice, be consistent throughout your work.

Think Before You Spell

I won't apologize for repeating that sound alone will not give you the most generally accepted spelling of a word. English is not the only language in which colloquial usage elides groups of words and in which vowel sounds are often slurred - more of a breath than a sound. But English seems to engender more spelling mistakes because of the difference between colloquial speech and written English.

The following common mistakes are due to the indefinite pronunciation of a vowel sound:

Wrong	Right
miniscule	minuscule
prosperus	prosperous
maintainence	maintenance
privilige	privilege
castor (sugar)	caster (sugar)
caster (oil)	castor (oil)
seperate	separate
superceed	supercede

The next list of mistakes stems from a mistake in the consonants.

accomodate	accommodate
concensus	consensus
exstacy	ecstacy
exeption	exception
millenium	millennium
Meditteranean	Mediterranean
Phillipine	Philippine
harrass	harass
embarass	embarrass

Sound again deceives us in the next group. These words, however, are less excusably mis-spelt because the right form is obvious if we trouble ourselves to remember the word from which they are formed. 'Accidently' is wrong because the adverb is made from the adjective 'accidental' and the adverb is then 'accidentally'. The adjective 'private' becomes 'privately' and 'public' becomes 'publicly'.

Finally, watch for those words which sound alike

A Fairly Straight and Narrow Path

but   have   very   different   meanings.   Go   to   the
dictionary, look them up and note down the meaning
of each one so that you never confuse them:

principle	principal
dependent	dependant
stationery	stationary
born	borne

8 THE ART OF DISTILLING

Precis and Summary: squashing and titbit picking

Fanny Cradock declares that currant buns taste
better if they are sat on before being eaten. The
flattened object is now the essence of currant bun
and compression has improved it. There would be
little point in writing at length if the expansion
of a topic did not, on the whole, enhance it. But
when space and time are short, content must be
squashed into a more manageable shape.

Learning how to sit on a topic without obscuring
its message may not appear to be very useful. The
sort of precis requirements of many examination
papers seem a long way from real life. Feverishly
counting words when a passage is to be reduced to
a given number of words feels to the candidate
like a waste of time. It is like those games where
one must find words of not fewer than three
letters in a slogan, save that there is no candy
bar at the end. The squashing of a passage, rather
than the quality of the work, seems to be the
reason for the exercise.

There are, however, good reasons for learning the
knack of precis-writing, apart from examination
marks. Brevity saves time. Note-taking is easier
and more effective if you can compress skilfully.
Research involving much reading is better done if

The Art of Distilling

you are already in the habit of selecting the important information in a text and know what is not
useful and can be discarded. And what may have
seemed a tedious and unamusing game at school may
prove to be a useful tool in employment for gain.
Until you become sufficently important to have
others do your reading for you, you may be your
own information-supplier, searching through papers
and documents, selecting the essentials for
someone else to ingest. How do you think that
chairmen of large companies and Cabinet Ministers
reel off facts and figures so confidently?
Dogsbodies garner the facts and figures from
sources the chairmen and Ministers have not time
to consult and present them in a form easily
mastered. This process enables even persons with
no professional knowledge of a department's work
or a subject to appear to understand it well.
Success depends on the quality of the precis.

Author, adviser, technical expert, student or
personal assistant to the great, the basic method
is the same for everyone. The precis must in-
corporate the salient facts from the original.
Examples, reasons and illustrations must be left
out unless they are providing necessary support
for a single conclusion. Details and descriptions
may be essential so their importance must be
assessed.

The beginning of the task is the identification of
the nature of the material to be condensed: description, narration, argument or reported action.
The first of these is an exercise in economy and
your choice of what is to remain depends on the
purpose of the precis. If you are only to present
a physical description of a man, then his visible
characteristics, from his height and weight to his
warts, are cogent facts. Should you want to show
his character, then the intangible factors like a
sense of humour, a gloomy outlook, extravagance,

The Art of Distilling

boastfulness and generosity help to depict a personality. A proper skeletal framework should be left when a narrative or part of a narrative is boiled down. Events should be in sequence and the thread of narrative unbroken. The reader will be confused if Friday's domestic accomplishments come before the discovery of his footprint. In collating and condensing documents and papers, selecting and abstracting, as well as arranging sequentially, are involved. The material may consist of fact, opinions and arguments. It is in making a precis of opinions and arguments that most care is needed.

The first step is to read and re-read the work you want to compress in order to determine the general intention of the writer and the principal topic. That done, you analyse the text, looking for what Wittgenstein calls "the atomic proposition". That is the simple unadorned statement on which the argument or opinion rests. Everything else only describes, supports or develops the proposition.

There is an underlying pattern in most written work, a thread of continuity, perhaps less visible in something that is badly written. Learn to recognize the pattern. In narrative pieces it is usual for the sequence of verbs to show the progress of narration:

        came, saw, conquered.

In arguments and the presentation of opinions and theories, the verbal sequence is not such a potent clue. The "atomic proposition" may be found after a preamble or a series of questioning statements which the proposition is to answer.

But the pattern of the work should show how the author is proceeding towards the proposition. After the essential statement has been found, the

The Art of Distilling

same may be re-argued and secondary statements supporting the main theme may have been added. Look for words that reinforce the proposition

so, thus, in this case, because,

and for words that show a change of direction or counter-argument:

but, on the other hand, if, however.

Make notes as you go. The impressions you get from your first reading may have to be revised, but they may also have been your instinctive recognition of what was important. They may also be useful in rewording - one is usually expected to write a precis in one's own words rather than the snappy phrases of the original.

Do not fall into despair and think that you must find a different word for every word used by the author. What you are doing is making the original briefer. By all means use the same words but do not necessarily use them in the same order. You are seeking constructions which can hold as much information as possible. 'Approve' can take the place of 'register approval of'. 'Ostentation' is an open display of wealth and extravagance and 'retrenchment' is what must follow an excess of expenditure over income as well as the action taken by the Chancellor of the Exchequer when the Treasury won't let him have as much money as he wants. 'Sordid' covers a multitude of sins. Words that can take the place of a whole group of words, a phrase or something expressed in several sentences, can be found. Making it a practice to consult a dictionary regularly should give you a useful vocabulary.

Words, and space, can be saved by careful reading. Many writers like an idea so much that they

The Art of Distilling

re-state it, in several different ways in the same paragraph or piece. A good eye for this sort of repetition can help you to lump all the good things into one sentence. If you have not reached your word limit and the precis looks a bit thin, choose the best of any examples or illustrations.

Beware, however, of the precis-writer's worst enemy - the convoluted argument. This is a much-used device in assessments and examinations of the Civil-Service sort. At first glance the argument appears to be in favour of the proposition. A second reading gives a negative impression - he is against the proposition. But a really careful analysis shows the depth of the writer's subtlety; the negative statements are really a form of devil's advocacy. They have been set up to demolish themselves. The counter-arguments only illustrate the weakness of any case against the proposition. The writer is whole-heartedly in favour of it. The satirical argument is a case in point. When Swift suggested that a remedy for poverty would be to eat the children of the poor, recommending boiled baby as a gourmet dish, he was, in reality, attacking attitudes to poverty which were, if less drastic, equally callous and cruel in their application.

The task is all the harder when the quantity of content in the text outweighs the quality. It is daunting to trudge through a superfluity of words, poured out over a trivial conclusion as a refuse truck empties its load onto the public tip. Grubbing through jargon and catchphrases ('at this moment in time' as if 'now' could be any other moment; 'in the last analysis' as if there had been dozens) is very boring, especially when all that is found is an opinion of little significance, but it must be done. Wordiness is not new. The essayists of the 18th and early 19th

The Art of Distilling

centuries were wordy in the extreme. Nevertheless they give us useful practice material. Read Hazlitt, Lamb, Kingslake, Stevenson and Macaulay. Hazlitt is a passionate critic, Lamb an observer of life and a philosopher, Kingslake's account of his journey through what was then the Turkish Empire is a classic narrative (it is also genuinely funny), Stevenson enjoyed quirkish propositions (spend money when you are young as you may not live to enjoy it) and Macaulay (the early 19th century equivalent of a good investigative reporter) used a study of a central character to comment generally on justice, society and the workings of an English government. Take a chunk from the middle of an essay by one of those writers and look for the central argument, the "atomic proposition"; then list all the statements that actively support it, examples, anecdotes and illustrations that clarify it and those words, phrases and sentences which are not really needed to do either. See if you can spot a negative argument and whether it is useful in establishing the truth of the proposition. Going through your listing, you make each item that supports the proposition or statement into a short sentence. Re-state the proposition in as few words as possible and arrange what you have written in one or two paragraphs. Only now need you start to count words and edit what you have written. Lambs' essay "A Chapter on Ears" can be reduced to one paragraph:

First Draft:

The writer says he has no ears. This is not meant in the physical sense; he has no ear for music. He is also tone-deaf and therefore finds concerts and professional performances, particularly concertos, painful and depressing. He is unusually susceptible to noise, even that of a carpenter's hammer. When he was young and sentimental he enjoyed hearing a woman sing, accompanying herself on the harpsicord. His friend Nov --- holds parties at which he plays the organ. Lamb enjoys the music at first, but finds too much of it overwhelming. He is glad when supper is served.

Second Draft:

Lamb claims to have no ear for music. He is tone-deaf, finding music played at concerts meaningless, painful and depressing, being distressed by noise of any kind. As a sentimental youth he enjoyed hearing a woman play the harpsicord and sing but when his friend Nov ---, playing the organ to his guests, goes on too long, pleasure turns to oppression and he welcomes the arrival of supper.

The original, Lamb's essay, is much better and full of humour. It also takes five pages.

The French words for 'editor' are 'redacteur' or 'redactrice', giving the sense of one of the most important editing acts: reduction. If you look at the two drafts above, you will see that many of the phrases and sentences in the first have been used in the second; it is only the words in between that have gone. As the number of words used was important, there have been some substitutions, but the second is largely faithful to the first. You can lift out a whole section of text in some circumstances, choosing sentences in an earlier paragraph which will run naturally on to a sentence in a later one without disturbing the sense or the message of the text. Some sentences can become clauses and add themselves to

others. Others, like superfluous words, can vanish
to the benefit of the text.

Nothing But the Truth — Salience and Summary

There may seem to be little difference between
precis-writing and summarizing. They are both
processes of abridgement and the dictionary defines a 'precis' as a 'summary'. When you are
asked to produce a summary, it may particularize
an aspect of the text. If a case or argument is
presented, you may need to summarize one or other
side of the argument. In a summary of narrative,
the action as it affects one character, or one
part of the action, could be required. You are not
just collecting all of the facts as a piece; you
are choosing those which are salient to the theme
of the summary. Here is a passage in full:

Powerboat Racing and Water-skiing

Powerboat racing, like water-skiing is most
attractive to its performers - but holds some
appeal for spectators. Powerboats need a large
area of water and from such boats there is a
risk of oil and petrol pollution which makes the
water unfit for swimming, while endangering the
fresh-water population. Powerboat enthusiasts
are represented by the RYA through their two
main membership groups: the Offshore Power Boat
Club of Great Britain and the United Kingdom
Offshore Boating Association. Like water-skiing
it is an expensive pastime, if one is going to
take it seriously, and acquires a bad name from
the inexperienced operator who hires a boat for
an afternoon's showing-off.

In a small country with an uncertain climate, it

The Art of Distilling

is hard to justify the designation of much
inland water for pursuits which have serious
disadvantages for other users. No one in his
senses would invite a friend from Italy or
Denmark to come here for the water-skiing; it is
too much like offering a Burgundy grower your
Dandelion brew. A rather chauvinist aura of
Olympic standards and the need to train for
international competitions hangs about
water-skiing, but it is a sport with few friends
outside its own devotees. Taking up the largest
amount of water for the fewest possible
participants, it erodes river banks, pollutes
with oil and petrol, disturbs people and birds
by its noise and totally eliminates all other
users from the water.

To keep the need for water-skiing areas in
perspective, it should be pointed out that there
are about 75,000 water-skiers in the whole
country; there are 175,000 adult members of the
Royal Society for the Protection of Birds and
there are 60,000 in the Young Ornithologists
Section and, of course, that does not include
the membership of the British Trust for
Ornithology, the British Naturalists'
Association, the Wildfowl Trust and the
Promotion of Nature Reserves which covers the
countless members of the County Naturalists'
Trusts. Anglers are counted by the million; with
ramblers and hikers, visitors and botanists,
these are some of the people whose leisure
enjoyment is at risk from the more energetic
water sports. Such comparative figures make
lobbying for more water for such pursuits not
merely inequitable but ridiculous. It is as if
shoppers' car parks were demanded for speedway
racing tracks.

The Art of Distilling

There is no doubt that some water should be
available for such sports; for the young,
fit and well-to-do expert it is ex-
hilarating. Even the risk of hitting the
water at 30 knots is part of the fun. They
are, however, already prepared to travel
some distance in search of an appropriate
arena; in some multi-use areas new courses
have been designed especially for them,
which reduce noise disturbance and allow
spectators some vicarious thrills. The
enjoyment and excitement it provides as a
performance is one of the positive aspects
of water-skiing. There is little doubt that
the Olympic standard courses at Holm
Pierrepoint and Thorpe will be watched by a
great many people and such places must cater
for spectators in their design. The
promotion of activities on a club basis has
made the organizing work of representative
bodies easier, particularly in terms of
demand for water use. It does, on the other
hand, mean a socio-economic inequity. No
matter what claims are put forward by the
CCPR or the Sports Council on their behalf,
users of all kinds do not get the same share
of that water. Public money spent on the
provision of recreation facilities must
benefit the solitary man and the more modest
forms of self-entertainment as well as those
of the more highly organized groups who can
afford club subscriptions.

Let us suppose that this is to be reduced in three
ways: precis, a summary of the arguments leading
to a recommended conclusion and a summary of the
points in favour of powerboating and water-skiing.
First, a quick precis:

Powerboating and water-skiing are noisy

expensive sports, contributing to
pollution and damaging the environment.
Although they attract spectators, the
number of participants is much smaller
than the number of people interested in
birds. Because demands for more water
space for these sports are made by clubs
promoting them, they carry unjustifiable
weight. The interest of solitary and
non-organized users is not so well
represented and their needs, when public
money is spent, must be seen as equally
important.

Now we can summarize the arguments of the piece.
The "atomic proposition" is contained in the last
sentence. As the arguments lead towards it, we can
leave it in that position and take them in order.

Powerboats and water-skiers need large areas
of water from which other users are excluded;

they are noisy activities, polluting water,
disturbing wildlife, causing bank damage and
endangering the freshwater population;

the number of participants is very small in
comparison with users having other interests
in inland waters;

the interests of the sports are promoted out
of proportion to the number taking part;

they take up an unfair share of available
water;

public money must be spent to benefit every
type and class of inland-water user.

And it is possible to find something agreeable to

The Art of Distilling

say about the sports:

> Powerboating and water-skiing are ex-
> hilarating sports, interesting the young and
> fit;

> people spend money on taking part and are
> prepared to travel some distance to do so;

> they are expensive, and, by inference, up-
> market sports;

> spectators enjoy them, particularly at
> Olympic-standard courses;

> because the sports are promoted by clubs,
> representative bodies are well-organized and
> form a powerful lobby.

You will see that both the summaries are presented
as lists. They are, in fact, unnumbered outlines.
The circumstances in which the summary is used
will dictate its shape. It may be necessary to
turn them into cohesive paragraphs. But the
outline form will always serve as an alternative,
even if you are running out of time. It is always
an easily-assimilated way of giving information to
someone else.

INDEX

Index

Index

Index

Index